Solving
Academic
and **Behavior**
Problems

Also by the Authors

Causes and Cures in the Classroom: Getting to the
Root of Academic and Behavior Problems
by Margaret Searle

Teacher Teamwork: How do we make it work?
(ASCD Arias)
by Margaret Searle and Marilyn Swartz

What Every School Leader Needs to Know About RTI
by Margaret Searle

Margaret Searle
Marilyn Swartz

Solving
Academic
and Behavior
Problems

A **Strengths-Based**
Guide for Teachers
and Teams

ASCD

Alexandria, Virginia USA

1703 N. Beauregard St. • Alexandria, VA 22311-1714 USA
Phone: 800-933-2723 or 703-578-9600 • Fax: 703-575-5400
Website: www.ascd.org • E-mail: member@ascd.org
Author guidelines: www.ascd.org/write

Ranjit Sidhu, *CEO & Executive Director*; Stefani Roth, *Publisher*; Genny Ostertag, *Director, Content Acquisitions*; Julie Houtz, *Director, Book Editing & Production*; Liz Wegner, *Editor*; Judi Connelly, *Senior Art Director*; Masie Chong, *Graphic Designer*; Keith Demmons, *Senior Production Designer*; Kelly Marshall, *Manager, Production Services*; Shajuan Martin, *E-Publishing Specialist*

The forms are available to download at www.ascd.org/ASCD/pdf/books/searleswartz2020.pdf.

All web links in this book are correct as of the publication date below but may have become inactive or otherwise modified since that time. If you notice a deactivated or changed link, please e-mail books@ascd.org with the words "Link Update" in the subject line. In your message, please specify the web link, the book title, and the page number on which the link appears.

PAPERBACK ISBN: 978-1-4166-2948-1   ASCD product #120016   n9/20
PDF E-BOOK ISBN: 978-1-4166-2963-4; see Books in Print for other formats.
Quantity discounts are available: e-mail programteam@ascd.org or call 800-933-2723, ext. 5773, or 703-575-5773. For desk copies, go to www.ascd.org/deskcopy.

Library of Congress Cataloging-in-Publication Data

Names: Searle, Margaret, author. | Swartz, Marilyn, author.
Title: Solving academic and behavior problems : a strengths-based guide for teachers and teams / Margaret Searle and Marilyn Swartz.
Description: Alexandria, Virginia : ASCD, [2020] | Includes bibliographical references and index.
Identifiers: LCCN 2020017474 (print) | LCCN 2020017475 (ebook) | ISBN 9781416629481 (paperback) | ISBN 9781416629634 (pdf)
Subjects: LCSH: Learning disabled children--Education--Case studies. | Response to intervention (Learning disabled children)--Case studies. | Behavior disorders in children--Treatment--Case studies.
Classification: LCC LC4704 .S44 2020 (print) | LCC LC4704 (ebook) | DDC 371.9--dc23
LC record available at https://lccn.loc.gov/2020017474
LC ebook record available at https://lccn.loc.gov/2020017475

29 28 27 26 25 24 23 22 21 20   1 2 3 4 5 6 7 8 9 10 11 12

To our grandchildren, Daphne, Julia, John Victor, Rebecca, Parker, and Kaia, and to all the children growing up with you, in hopes that this book helps create a more positive world for you to learn and grow in.

Solving Academic and Behavior Problems

Foreword

There's an old joke that defines a consultant as a person who looks at your watch and tells you what time it is. As a consultant, I can tell you that the joke isn't as derogatory as you might think. After reading Margaret Searle and Marilyn Swartz's book, I'm convinced that they would agree that the main role of a good consultant is not to introduce novel solutions but rather to encourage people to look at their watches—to help organizations recognize the potential that's already in their own hands.

Solving Academic and Behavior Problems offers schools a highly effective way to harness their potential through a strengths-based approach to solving academic and social-emotional problems. This approach is predicated on the belief that when people deliberately examine their own past successes, they are able to abstract principles to apply to new challenges. You can test this premise in a very basic way right now. For example, think of a time you were able to motivate a child who was resistant to learning. What did you do? What happened as a result? Are there any takeaways from this experience that you might be able to apply in the future? By helping teachers identify their most important concerns and examine previous successes with students, Searle and Swartz have tapped into a great source of power. In short, they have shown educators how to use their past and their present to improve their students' futures.

The book reveals to educators a clear path to improved teaching and learning based on the appreciative inquiry approach to problem solving. Adapted from the work of David Cooperrider and Suresh Srivastva at Case Western Reserve University, the appreciative inquiry approach is one that honors what we already do. It recognizes that we all have practices that work for us, and it helps us to get even more out of those practices. Through the act of reflecting on our experiences and zeroing in on what works, we can develop solutions to our most pressing problems. This approach invites us to pose questions, analyze what is currently producing positive results, set meaningful and manageable goals, and develop action plans to achieve those goals.

With this strengths-based mindset as their guide, Searle and Swartz show educators how to apply the techniques in real schools. The book is filled with tools and strategies for promoting constructive conversations about problems that educators care about and for working cooperatively and strategically to address real classroom challenges. One of these practical tools is the strength chart, which, as the authors demonstrate clearly, can affect the individual student, the classroom, and the entire school culture. How? By breaking down social-emotional learning, motivation, and academic skills with a level of specificity that makes it easy for students and their teachers to celebrate strengths and identify opportunities for growth. Strength charts promote a common language that ensures that teachers and students can communicate effectively with each other. This common language can become a linchpin of collaboration among members of the school community, thus supporting shared responsibility for every child.

Over the course of the book, the authors expand their vision outward so that strengths-based thinking guides the school as a whole. Searle and Swartz demonstrate how teachers can use strengths-based practices to become more effective coaches for one another. They lay out how teams can conduct successful strengths-based meetings to reduce stress and improve practice. Instead of conducting meetings that are seen by staff as unproductive, you can apply the wisdom of this book and turn meetings into strengths-based team conversations that address real concerns, lead to practical strategies, and produce results in classroom instruction.

As I see it, *Solving Academic and Behavior Problems* is an important book on its own, as well as part of a larger—and very welcome—movement that is helping today's educators to take control over their challenges by looking for bright spots and natural sources of strength to focus their energy. If you are a teacher looking for a proven way to help and inspire more students, a coach searching for more effective practices to support teachers, or a school leader working to create positive, systemwide change, then this book is for you. It is a book of *wish craft*—a way to craft, or to make real, our most important wishes for our students.

—Harvey F. Silver

Introduction: A Support System That Works

Has your classroom ever resembled this? Lamar is trying hard but cannot remember what we did yesterday. Sonia is out of her seat again, vying for attention by bothering Zach. Omaldo just snapped his pencil in two and called Tony a jerk.

These students didn't get their work completed, and no wonder. They are having a hard time feeling successful at school. Each one has a unique way of learning, very different background knowledge, and a distinct way of demonstrating the frustrations they feel.

This book is about discovering the keys that open doors to student success, as well as finding ways to engage school personnel, families, and students in taking advantage of new academic and social-emotional learning opportunities. We know that the best results happen when home and school work together to establish the right conditions for success. Success is more likely when we all start with the belief that people are knowledgeable, capable, and willing to learn, even when their outward behavior seems to indicate they are not. Thinking that a given teacher will never change or that a specific student doesn't care can result in feelings of helplessness and hopelessness—and *that* results in lack of action. Believing that there is a hot button that will turn failures into successes is fundamental to being successful. The tricky part is finding those hot buttons.

Some people think that testing, labeling, and dispatching a student to someone else's roster is the hot button. We have all heard adults ask, "Why are we wasting time doing all these interventions and holding all these meetings when we know this kid needs to be tested?" The belief underlying this statement is that testing and placement are interventions. They're not.

Testing provides data but not answers. Labeling only gives the problem a name; it doesn't provide support. And placement often only moves the challenge to a new location or person. Although many people believe that intensive one-to-one assistance occurs in special education classrooms, that is typically a myth. Yes, special education teachers have fewer students than general education teachers do, but the complexity of those students' needs is far more intense. The paperwork, scheduling, and class structures for special education teachers can be insane. Too often the tasks of reading tests aloud, helping with homework, and getting students to fix or complete missed class assignments eat up most of the intervention time, making the kind of support students really need difficult to deliver. This outdated model often results in widening the achievement gap rather than providing a successful tailor-made learning experience that is continuously monitored and adjusted. We need a new model for solving these problems.

A Quick Walk Through the Book

In each of the chapters that follow, we describe a system of support that helps general education teachers partner with specialists and parents to learn new ways to enrich academic, social-emotional, and behavioral growth. This model is designed to fit into and enhance the existing structures of teacher meetings. It also provides ongoing support to help teachers apply an ounce of prevention in the classroom before the pound of cure is necessary.

Chapter 1 provides an overview of how the positive psychology of *appreciative inquiry* changes the way we look at student problems. Instead of using the deficit model of fixing what's wrong, our method builds on what is currently working to address what is not. This approach is successfully being used worldwide in industry and medicine to cultivate optimism, build capacity, and unleash creative thinking that brings about positive change. It's time to apply this approach to education.

Chapter 2 suggests a technique for rolling out this new strengths-based model in a way that makes teacher team meetings proactive and productive. By using a basic set of positive questions, teams quickly address their top Tier 1 concerns by implementing action plans put together in a single meeting. This builds a database of intervention strategies that people have confidence in.

Chapter 3 addresses the problem of how to strengthen parent and student involvement in a way that benefits the students you worry about most. A quick and easy interview process will turn tedious intervention planning into a shorter and more effective experience. These

15-minute conversations with parents and students improve motivation and follow-through, as well as provide insights to teachers about the whole child.

Chapter 4 discusses how to reduce paperwork and jumping through hoops as teachers seek help from a coach to better address the needs of struggling students in Tiers 2 and 3. The process is about changing student lives through quick and specific support sessions for teachers. Each session results in an action plan. If evidence from that plan does not show positive movement, the plan is quickly adjusted or replaced with a better one. This process goes on until the student succeeds or graduates, whichever comes first. We never give up or settle.

Chapter 5 discusses what to do when the procedures we have described don't show satisfactory results. In these cases, we add a step called *five whys*. Five whys is a Toyota quality tool for drilling down to a root cause; we use it to pinpoint what missing skill the student needs. This process uncovers hidden barriers that need to be addressed so students can move forward.

Chapter 6 gives specific steps and models for holding student support team meetings in 25 minutes and walking out with an action plan every time. Parents and students are included in this conversation, so all students have voice and choice, which keeps their motivation high. The goal is to surround students with support from the significant people in their lives.

Chapter 7 addresses frequently asked questions, such as how to structure and roll out the process in your school and how to get teacher, student, and parent buy-in. Each chapter in the book contains activities, video examples, scenarios, and tips from practitioners in the field to help you develop your skills as a potential coach and problem solver. The forms that appear throughout this book are also available at www.ascd.org/ASCD/pdf/books/searleswartz2020 .pdf.

So let's get started. The Lamars, Sonias, and Omaldos of our world are counting on us!

A New Lens for
Solving Old Problems

It was a chilly February morning and I, Margaret, was to spend three days at a school that served 90 percent struggling learners. The principal described the emotional situation as "intense" due to a huge reduction in both services and resources the previous December. Feeling beaten up by their daily stresses, faculty members were losing their motivation to work together as a team. Meetings had deteriorated into complaining sessions, and the staff was using sick days like crazy. Working harder was impossible, and so were the demands of the job. My job as a visiting consultant was to help teachers figure out what to do about the wide variety of academic and social-emotional needs of their students without sending the teachers over their mental edge.

To clarify the type of support needed, consultants often begin by asking, "What can I do to help you?" This typically works like a charm for identifying the needs and goals for the session. This time it didn't. Every time I asked that question, teachers launched into an emotional enumeration of problems and stressors they could no longer tolerate. Because venting is only helpful in small doses, I didn't wait long to put the positive psychology research I had been reading about to the test. We needed a new approach for solving these old problems.

I asked each teacher, "Which problem would you like to tackle first?" Then, to switch the conversation to a positive lens, I asked the teachers to tell me about a time when they experienced the same problem but were able to turn the situation around, even if it was only for a day or just a few minutes. As teachers detailed their successful experiences, I asked them to elaborate on exactly what they did to make that success possible, as well as what the students did in response. Each teacher was able to identify things that worked with the class or student in question. Every conversation took on a more helpful and creative quality as the teachers focused on what had worked in the past. You could see and feel tension dissolve and a spark of hopefulness ignite. I began to understand the true power of appreciative inquiry and what it can produce.

Appreciative inquiry is based on the belief that focusing on strengths and on what is going well results in a more positive and creative approach to solving sticky problems. So if strengths-based approaches are so powerful, why the continued focus on the deficit problem-solving model?

What's Wrong with a Deficit Approach?

There is nothing inherently wrong with it. For hundreds of years, people have successfully used the process of identifying what is wrong, analyzing why an issue continues to be a problem, and deciding on ways to fix it. However, even when it is used with the best of intentions, the unintended consequences of this model are the defensive feelings it can stir up. As people become more defensive, the problem-solving part of their brain shuts down as strong feelings and emotions take over, thus stifling creativity, open-mindedness, and logical decision making. This type of response makes progress more difficult to achieve. Therefore, when beginning these problem-solving conversations, we suggest adding another approach—appreciative inquiry—to your tool kit.

How Is Appreciative Inquiry Different?

Formalized by David Cooperrider and Suresh Srivastva in 1987 at Case Western Reserve University, appreciative inquiry is a positive psychology approach to change that has been practiced around the world for more than a decade by nonprofit organizations, Fortune 500 companies, health care agencies, schools, and governments. Positive psychology is based on the premise that more energy is directed to the thinking part of our brains when we focus on strengths, goals, and what is going well. This doesn't mean we stick our head in the sand and refuse to acknowledge problems. It means that how we frame a problem makes a difference in our level of resilience and openness.

For example, instead of asking why 24 percent of our students are unable to read on grade level, it would be better to ask, "What are we doing that enables 76 percent of our students to be successful readers, and what do the other students need more of?" Students and staff are typically willing to listen to and engage in telling success stories that verify what teachers, parents, and students know are practices that will positively influence their situation. These stories enable them to identify ways to increase what is working well and identify what they need to add to the mix.

Cooperrider, Whitney, and Stavros (2003) argued that we tend to get more of whatever we pay attention to, so talking about what is already right generates the confidence and motivation we need to expand and replicate these good practices in new situations. Affirming and building on strengths that already exist open us to new levels of energy and possibilities for overcoming obstacles. Positive feelings enable us to be more flexible, creative, and efficient in our thinking (Isen & Reeve, 2005).

Here are the six basic steps to the appreciative inquiry approach that we will cover in this book:

1. **Connect:** Begin by asking a question designed to establish a positive tone and build relationships among team members. Ask participants to share funny anecdotes or interesting things about themselves. This establishes the right frame of mind for doing hard work.

2. **Review the concern/focus:** Clearly state what needs to be accomplished.

3. **Share success stories:** Get team members to recount stories that reveal what has been successful for them in the past. This positive core of the process builds a can-do environment and reveals values and strengths to build on.

4. **Establish a DATA goal:** Forge a statement that clarifies what we will do differently to achieve the desired end result, the time frame, and the specifics for measuring growth.

5. **Design an action plan:** Come up with an action plan listing what people will do to create a successful experience.

6. **Commit to an action:** Make a specific commitment to start right away with small steps that will begin to make the vision a reality.

These steps don't always follow this order, but together they result in an energetic strengths-based conversation that pays off with an action plan at the end.

The questions asked are the heart of this process. The stories told are the soul that gives meaning and substance to the plans. The commitment serves as the launching pad that gets everything moving quickly. Olin Miller once said, "If you want to make an easy job seem hard, just keep putting it off." Ending each conversation with a commitment to get started the next day keeps difficult jobs from becoming overwhelming.

Team Meetings—Transformed

Do teachers in your building say things like, "I get more done when I figure out how to avoid our team meetings" or "We sit around and admire data and problems for hours. When are we going to do something important that changes our results?" One teacher I met quipped that he hoped when he died it would be during a staff meeting—because it would make the transition so subtle. If meetings at your school are coma-inducing and unmotivating, perhaps it's time to change your approach.

Meetings should be compelling, creative, and intense, not boring and unproductive. They must address pressing issues the team cares about, as well as energize people to achieve worthwhile things. Support and commitment don't just happen, even when you work with competent and caring people. They take intentional plans, constructive conversations, and good meeting protocols.

Most well-intended school improvement plans focus on what needs to be fixed. This makes sense because that is how we have done business for hundreds of years: Tell me what's wrong, then we'll figure out why that is happening and look at options for fixing it. This can work, but it often generates pushback from the people who are required to implement a plan in which they have had limited input. Sometimes they don't even think that what you are fixing is a real problem.

Appreciative inquiry is built on the premise that every system and person has things that already work for them. When we focus on what works and what is going right, we can use those ideas to develop ways to improve. This strengths-based approach engages the primary stakeholders in asking questions, analyzing what is currently working, setting new goals, and developing action plans for achieving those goals.

What we focus on gets stronger. Alternatively, when we choose to focus on uncooperative students and daily stresses, they loom even larger. Have you ever gone into the teachers' lounge feeling OK, only to hear one person after another complain about how intolerable the kids and conditions are? If other people join in and add to that poisonous conversation, you leave feeling drained.

The team meetings we describe in this book start by asking the teachers to identify three key concerns that stand in the way of many students' success. Teachers have no problem making lists of things they wish they could change: students' lack of organization, poor motivation, inability to comprehend text, or failure to complete homework, to name a few. Addressing these teacher-identified issues becomes the content of the agendas for two teacher meetings each month. Because the teachers have a voice in setting the agendas, it creates a sense of ownership in the meetings and more motivation to get things done.

Scheduling topics that teachers want to discuss is half the task. The other half is making sure the conversation about concerns doesn't becoming a griping and blaming session. Again, it's all about crafting the right questions. Appreciative inquiry questions empower people by eliciting success stories that are described in enough detail to clarify the vision and switch perspectives to enable new possibilities. A key person in this process is the coach.

The Role of the Coach

The coaching role can be filled by anyone on the staff who is a good listener with a positive outlook when solving problems. This can be an administrator, a counselor, a specialist, or a classroom teacher. When starting off, choose a set of people who show interest in coaching and who are seen by the faculty as trustworthy and helpful.

To foster successful, strengths-based conversations, every coach needs to be skilled at the following:

1. Be a good listener and observer so you can reflect people's strengths, best practices, and fresh solutions back to them. You will need to be able to capture both their thoughts and feelings as you paraphrase what you hear them say so you can reframe their thinking in a larger vision.

2. Ask questions that focus on assets and opportunities instead of on weaknesses and problems.

3. Help people feel safe, valued, and welcome to release their creative thinking. An environment of trust is essential.

4. Invite people to commit to excellence instead of business as usual.

5. Use the five whys questioning technique (more on this shortly) to identify hidden skill needs.

6. Be familiar with the strength charts we provide in this book to help teachers articulate specific areas of strength and what students need more of.

You can start to develop these skills by using the practice videos and activities we provide here. However, reading about the process, watching demonstrations, and discussing only take you part of the way. It's like learning to swim; you have to jump into the pool and do the hard work if you want to become proficient. This will take consistent practice over time, but it's worth every minute spent. That is why we offer such a wide variety of activities to guide you through the steps.

Let's look at a tool called *strength charts* now; these will make the process much easier.

Strength Charts: How Can They Help?

A strength chart is a listing of desirable assets arranged by categories to help you identify student strengths and opportunities for improvement. To demonstrate the thinking behind this tool, let's say you have decided to design a health improvement plan for yourself. You know you want good health, but it is hard to decide where to start. Begin by thinking of subcategories like nutrition, exercise, stress, and sleep. We can evaluate which of these are strong areas for you and which ones you need to improve.

Let's say you're a runner, and you work out at the gym twice a week. Obviously, this is a strength. You also know your eating habits include lots of snacks but few fruits and vegetables. Now there's an opportunity. Breaking down the big category of health into subcategories was helpful, but breaking these subcategories into smaller subskills makes it easier to identify where to start on your improvement plan.

When designing a support plan, teachers and coaches sometimes find it hard to articulate a list of subskills that the student already has and ones that are priority needs. For instance, say you want a student to become more resilient. Can you list 10 skills a resilient person possesses? Which of the skills listed are the strongest for this student, and which ones need work? How about 10 skills for a creative writer? The charts in this book—there are 16 in all, and you can find them in Appendix A beginning on page 154—will help you through this conversation. A chart is available for each major academic, social-emotional, and executive function category. You will find charts on math, reading, and writing, as well as on such categories as memory, resilience, organization, problem solving, and self-regulation.

A Word About Executive Function

Many of the strength charts we include deal specifically with executive function skills because they are so crucial to school success. Neurologists use the term *executive function* to describe brain processes that drive our ability to focus, solve problems, organize, remember, self-monitor, and control our impulses, all of which help us learn efficiently and develop important social skills (Blair, 2002). Understanding how executive function skills develop helps parents and educators pinpoint the best responses to academic and behavior problems that are often mistaken for laziness, carelessness, or lack of motivation.

Contrary to popular belief, executive function skills—especially working memory—rather than IQ are the best predictor of success in reading, spelling, and math (Alloway & Alloway, 2010). Teachers often believe that students struggle because of lack of focus or low IQ; seldom do they identify working memory or other executive function skills as the most crucial learning opportunity. However, when teachers integrate executive function and social-emotional skills in daily lessons, students are more prone to develop flexible, adaptive responses to demands. They learn how to recognize and manage their emotions and stress, set positive goals, appreciate the perspective of others, maintain concern for others, make responsible decisions, handle interpersonal situations constructively, and take responsibility for their choices (see CASEL's *Framework for Systemic Social and Emotional Learning*, 2005). For more information on executive function skills and the interventions that help develop them, refer to *Causes and Cures in the Classroom: Getting to the Root of Academic and Behavior Problems* (Searle, 2013).

How the Strength Charts Are Organized

As we compiled these charts, we started by identifying the subcategories under each major academic, social-emotional, or executive function area. Then we researched the most important strengths a person needs to be effective in this category.

Each chart deals with a specific category. For instance, consider the strength chart on problem solving shown in Figure 1.1. The boxes directly under the main heading divide the chart into broad areas of competence. In the case of problem solving, three broad areas are listed: Defines the Problem, Creates a Plan, and Assesses and Adjusts. Under these categories are subcategories that describe specific skills in terms of "I statements"; these may be a strength for a student or an area of need.

Let's say the teacher has this to say about a student: "Juan is an enthusiastic starter, but he gives up after he meets the first bump in the road." A coach selects the most useful chart that will help him or her diagnose the problem. Often, several charts fit equally well, so a coach may start with multiple charts and then narrow down the possibilities as the conversation progresses. In Juan's case, the coach decides to use the problem-solving strength chart.

The coach starts by asking which skills in the area of "Creates a Plan" Juan applies well. If the teacher says that Juan is good at organizing steps (the second item in the column) and that he schedules his time well (the fourth item in the column), two strengths are identified that the teacher can build on. The teacher may now consider other areas—such as looking for patterns, considering pros and cons, and anticipating roadblocks—as potential new learning opportunities.

Obviously, these charts cannot list all the possible skills of any category, but they do get the conversation started and make the diagnosis of needs more specific. As teachers think of additional skills that fit the case, they can add them to their own charts.

FIGURE 1.1

Strength Chart on Problem Solving

Problem Solving		
Defines the Problem	**Creates a Plan**	**Assesses and Adjusts**
I break down big goals or problems into smaller and more manageable parts.	I set realistic goals for myself.	I use models, rubrics, and checklists to self-assess my work.
I can visualize and explain what things should look like or sound like when I'm finished.	I sequence what I need to do by how important it is or what needs to be done first.	I collect data and get feedback on how well my plan is working and use them to improve my plan.
I figure out what information I have that is useful and what information I still need.	I look for patterns that have helped me in the past.	I keep a list of strategies and resources that work for me.
I can restate the problem or expectations in my own words.	I estimate how long things will take and create a timeline that I check regularly.	I stop to celebrate small successes along the way.
When I am solving problems, I can identify what is going well and what I don't understand.	I think of pros and cons of solutions before I decide what to do.	I see mistakes and setbacks as things to learn from, and I don't give up.
	I anticipate roadblocks and have backup options in case I need them.	I can explain how my effort, skills, strategies, and decisions determine my success.

How to Use the Strength Charts

Now that you know the purpose of strength charts, let's take a look at various ways to use them.

To Encourage Student Self-Assessment

These charts make it easier for teachers and coaches to help students identify their areas of strength as well as opportunities for growth. In the world of sports, athletes and their coaches often have these same types of conversations. For example, a tennis coach might ask new players to identify what they are already good at and what they need help with. Experienced players may easily articulate their strengths and needs. However, inexperienced players typically have more difficulty accurately describing their level of performance because they don't know the key subskills required to play well. A chart of desired competencies makes this self-assessment far easier.

To Give Quality Feedback

A tennis coach who gives players feedback by saying, "You're excellent at playing tennis" hasn't said anything helpful. An effective coach might say, "You have a strong forehand, and your serving and footwork are solid, too. Now we're going to work on your topspin because that helps keep the ball inside the court." This clear and specific feedback on explicit skills gives the student both encouragement and direction for further growth.

To Help Parents Provide Background Information

Getting to know the whole child is a huge advantage in developing positive relationships and building quality support plans. There isn't a better source for getting background knowledge than talking to both the student and his or her parents or caregivers. When teachers ask parents to name their child's strengths, the list they provide is always interesting and often different from what a teacher sees. If the parent describes their child as being organized, it is helpful and eye-opening to pull out the strength chart on organization (see Appendix A) and have them identify the precise skills they see at home that make them see organization as their child's strength. At the end of the conversation, many parents say that using the charts helped them appreciate their child in a new way. They may also use the charts to select a skill for improvement that will take their child to a new level of competence.

Five Whys Conversations

Because the skills on one chart overlap and extend those from other charts, coaches typically use several charts as resources for describing what is in place and what the next steps should be. This is especially true during five whys conversations.

Five whys is a Six Sigma tool developed by Toyota for problem solving. During this diagnostic conversation, a coach begins by asking the teacher why a certain problem is occurring; after each reason the teacher gives, the coach asks another why question. This process is a little bit like the one your 3-year-old uses that drives you nuts, but it's a wonderful tool for seeing below the surface of an issue you cannot figure out. Coaches are trained to go a minimum of five levels deep because experience shows that unexpected root causes or skill needs generally don't show up until the questions go that far. Chapter 5 provides lots of examples and practice scenarios to help you learn how to use the five whys process.

Sometimes a coach will ask a teacher, "Why do you think *X* is happening?" and the teacher can't come up with an answer. Sometimes the coach gets as stuck as the teacher is—and that's when the coach pulls out the strength charts to help.

Because these charts list competencies necessary for effective performance, they also serve to identify gaps that impede that performance, hence the root cause of a problem. We strongly suggest that the coach not use the charts until at least three why questions have been asked because it's unwise to skew the teacher's thinking by offering a list too soon.

In Activity 1, you will see how using multiple charts can be helpful. In this case study, we will use the motivation and problem solving charts. In reality, additional charts would probably be just as helpful.

Activity 1. How to Use the Strength Charts

Read the following case study. Use the strength chart on problem solving shown in Figure 1.1 on page 8 and the one on motivation shown in Figure 1.2 to determine strengths and learning opportunities for Seth. Keep in mind that a chart's title and headings are not specific enough to be helpful. Look at the list of specific skills phrased as "I statements" listed under the various headings.

Seth has good attendance, reads well, and is well liked by teachers and other students. His math teacher initiated a coaching conversation because he is only completing about 60 percent of his assignments on time. His science teacher sees a similar pattern. However, he is doing very well with assignments in his English and social studies classes.

When the math teacher assesses him orally, Seth has no problem restating the problem in his own words. He is also quick to pick up on when his answer doesn't

FIGURE 1.2

Strength Chart on Motivation

Motivation			
Sees How a Task Is Relevant	**Accurately Assesses Strengths and Needs**	**Sees How Effort Affects Success**	**Contributes to a Positive Environment**
I can tell others the importance and usefulness of the work I do.	I know my own strengths and use them to learn more.	I accurately estimate how much time and effort I need to be successful.	I recognize ways to show respect and acceptance for teachers and the group.
I choose to do challenging work because I know that taking reasonable risks helps me learn more.	I know what skills I need to work on, and I make plans for ways to improve.	I try to solve problems on my own first and know ways to get help when I cannot.	I make sure others' ideas and feelings are accepted and respected.
I work to meet my goals instead of working just for rewards, grades, and praise.	I know a variety of creative ways to approach learning and problem solving.	I look for a variety of ways to practice to improve my skills.	I help my group get things done by working together.
I see how my effort and use of good strategies affect my own success.	I ask for help and feedback when I need it and know the right ways to ask.	I keep a list of strategies that do and do not work for me.	I ask for and use feedback and ideas for improving my skills and work.
I see how what I am learning can be helpful outside school.	I track my own growth so I know when to keep doing what I am doing and when to ask for help.	I use visual displays of my own growth to know when to adjust my strategies.	I thank people for a job well done and give helpful hints for improving things.

make sense. He immediately tries a different way of approaching the solution and is genuinely excited if his new way works.

The math teacher says Seth has a hard time staying focused when he doesn't get the answer right away. He works for five or six minutes and then stops. When the teacher asks if he needs help, he says no, but then he just sits there doing nothing. His mother said Seth hates math, that he's hated it for the last two years. He complains a lot about being bored. She is worried about Seth's attitude about school in general.

According to Seth, school was easy for him in the lower grades, but now it's so much harder. He told his dad that he is not so sure that he is as smart as everyone thinks he is.

Now, before reading on, list the top items from each chart that you consider to be Seth's strengths and needs. Naturally, you can't be sure your analysis is correct without actually talking to Seth, his parents, and his teacher, but choose the most likely answers from these two charts.

Seth: What the Charts Reveal

Seth seems discouraged by the fact that school used to be easy and now it requires a lot of effort. This is what Carol Dweck (2016) refers to as signs of a *fixed mindset*. Fixed mindset students think that if you have to try hard, you are not smart. Alternatively, *growth mindset* students think that trying hard makes you smarter.

Seth has many strengths that are not listed on the two charts we selected. His reading skill, his attendance record, and his social skills are all important strengths. The fact that he is getting his assignments in on time in social studies and English eliminates some of the issues that originally looked like areas of need.

We can see that on the problem solving chart, under "Defines the Problem," Seth can restate the problem in his own words. He also can identify what's going well and what doesn't make sense. These are strengths. As far as needs are concerned, looking at that same column, it's possible that seeing all the work as one huge task is overwhelming for Seth in math and science. Breaking down his to-do list into more manageable pieces may help him reduce his stress. Under "Assesses and Adjusts," seeing setbacks as learning opportunities may help him feel less like giving up.

Now let's take a look at the motivation chart. Under "Accurately Assesses Strengths and Needs," Seth is able to use a variety of creative approaches. Under "Contributes to a Positive Environment," he seems to show respect and acceptance for teachers and classmates because he is well liked by both. Both of these are strengths. However, in the area of "Sees How a Task Is Relevant," he doesn't seem to understand how challenging work helps him learn more, and under

"Accurately Assesses Strengths and Needs," it's possible that either he can't articulate what he needs help with or he is too embarrassed to ask.

As you worked through Seth's case, you may have eliminated or added possibilities not listed here. There are no correct or incorrect answers; there are only possibilities based on the evidence you have. This is a starting place; you will deepen your understanding through a series of conversations with his teachers, his parents, and Seth himself.

Activity 2. Using the Five Whys: Celina's Case

Celina is a freshman at Milbourne High School. According to her teacher, Celina cares about success. She wants a job as an office helper in the school, but she has to meet criteria involving grades and behavior to get it. She is bright and can handle most of the work, but she gets frustrated and walks out of class at least three times a week. She is pleasant to talk to when she's not upset, and she has several good friends. She is not afraid to express her opinion or to stick up for herself when she thinks she's right. She reads and writes fairly well, but persistence is a problem.

At their initial meeting, the coach and teacher used appreciative inquiry to create a plan for building Celina's ability to persist. They started by identifying her strengths and needs using the strength chart on resilience and flexibility (see Appendix A). The new skill they decided to teach her was "I stop and think of options before I act or give up." That action plan made some difference for Celina, but it wasn't enough.

Some cases are too complex to be solved by simply looking at the strength charts because the root cause is not obvious. In these cases, we insert the five whys conversation into the process before developing a new action plan. (We'll walk you through the five whys process in more detail in Chapter 5, but here's a sneak peek at what it looks like.)

What follows is the five whys conversation between the problem-solving coach and Kaia, Celina's English teacher. After reading the case study, use a strength chart to complete an analysis and action plan for Celina.

Coach: Why does Celina walk out of class?

Kaia: She gets upset when things don't come easy for her.

Coach: Why does that upset her so much that she leaves?

Kaia: Actually, anything can set her off. It seems like she is always looking for a reason to run.

Coach: So she avoids situations where she's uncomfortable?

Kaia: Most of the time. But if you confront her, she will lash out. She's always on edge.

Coach: What causes her to be so on edge?

Kaia: She's had a hard life at home, and I know that is out of my circle of influence, but it's a big factor.

Coach: Even though her home situation is out of our influence, school stress is not, so let's see if we can drill down deeper and figure out what causes that edginess at school and what skills we can put in place to help her cope.

Kaia: I've read that children who have experienced trauma are often on high alert most of the time for anything that might threaten them. I suppose that fits what I see in Celina, but I don't know what to do for her.

Coach: Children who have lived with trauma need trusting relationships. You are great at doing that, and we can put together a team to provide even more strategies. That won't be enough, however, because when you're not around to support her, Celina will need her own set of coping skills. Let's look at the strength chart on resilience and flexibility and see which skills she has in place and which ones we need to help her with.

As you consider this scenario, how would you complete the following prompts? Reference the strength charts and use these questions to help with your analysis and action plan for Celina.

- Strengths Celina can build on:
- Skills that would help her cope with her stress:
- Suggestions you could give to Kaia that would help:

In a Nutshell

In the process that we have just laid out, teachers and coaches go beyond talking about academic and behavior problems to look at what social-emotional and executive function skills—or lack thereof—lie behind the symptoms seen in the classroom. Research (Durlak, Weissberg, Dymnicki, Taylor, & Schellinger, 2011) shows that programs focusing on social-emotional outcomes demonstrate improvement in behavior, attendance, and academic performance. Consistent support for areas of social-emotional growth gets results in all academic areas. Using appreciative inquiry helps teachers and parents look at the whole child before designing action plans.

When groups or individuals use an appreciative inquiry format to discuss problems, they are more likely to see challenging issues as opportunities for growth. By reflecting on what goes well when students are at their best, teachers can see new ways of applying these same strategies to difficult situations. In Chapter 2, we'll look at the nuts and bolts of using appreciative inquiry in teacher meetings to create targeted action plans for groups of students in Tier 1 classroom instruction.

Strengths-Based Team Conversations

Research shows that 46 percent of teachers perceive their occupation as routinely creating high to very high levels of stress for them (Greenberg, Brown, & Abenavoli, 2016). High daily stress compromises a teacher's health, sleep, quality of life, and teaching performance. Such stress may account for the fact that between 40 to 50 percent of our teachers leave the profession within the first five years (Ingersoll, 2012), costing states up to $2 billion (Neason, 2014) each year.

But the real question is, what about those stressed teachers who stay? Research (Greenberg et al., 2016) shows that high stress levels in teachers affect both student social adjustment and academic performance. Knowing this, do you want your child being taught by a teacher who is in a state of chronic stress? We need to do all we can to reduce the anxiety levels of the faculty if we want our children to receive the kind of educational experience every parent hopes for.

When we asked teachers and administrators what types of things increase their stress levels, they had no problem creating a list (see Figure 2.1). This chart lists teacher stressors, the strategies we suggest that help, and the reason each strategy is effective. Note the importance of working as a team using structured protocols as an effective antidote for teacher stress.

FIGURE 2.1

Teacher Stressors and Suggested Solutions

Teacher Stressor	Strategy	Why It Works
"I often feel isolated and over-whelmed. After I was hired, I was welcomed, shown my room, given my materials, and left to fend for myself. I wish I had someone I could go to without feeling like I'm an incompetent pest."	Holding regular team meetings designed to address concerns and share successful strategies	Meetings that are structured to provide embedded professional development help build capacity in everyone and reduce feelings of isolation and frustration.
"We want data-driven decision making, but I don't know what data to collect or how to collect them. Sometimes it feels like I spend more time testing and compiling data than I do teaching."	Clarifying problems and identify-ing progress monitoring tools for measuring growth	The team develops ways of collect-ing data that are short, quick, and usable for classroom instruction the very next day.
"People are reluctant to share strategies for fear of being viewed as a know-it-all, having others take credit for their work, or having their ideas criticized."	Using a strengths-based model for regular team discussions	The norm becomes regular sharing of successful strategies and building capacity in one another so every teacher is better equipped to sup-port all types of learners.
"Our staff feels like things keep being added to our plates, and we have very little say about it. It's just overwhelming. We've lost our voice as educators."	Holding strengths-based teacher meetings	Teams regain their voice about ways to make the biggest difference in student learning. They learn to trust that their group can develop solu-tions to low performance and other urgent and important problems.

It All Starts with Successful Meeting Practices

Parker, the new 6th grade math teacher at Wagner Middle School, was the talk of the first administrative meeting. The school had hired a rising star. He was enthusiastic, he asked the right questions, and the kids took to him immediately. His lesson plans were thorough, and his classroom hummed with "learning noise" without being chaotic. What administrator wouldn't be proud of this new hire?

By February, however, Parker was feeling isolated and frustrated; he was even talking about leaving the teaching profession to become a pharmaceutical representative like his brother.

Fortunately, an 8th grade teacher, Mary, caught wind of this and started informally touching base with him at lunch. They agreed to meet every Tuesday so Parker could discuss problems and ask questions. They reflected on and learned from what went right and wrong in both of their classes, and they shared successful strategies. Both teachers grew to genuinely enjoy these luncheon meetings, and the energy they created drew other people into their discussions. Within six weeks, Parker had regained his enthusiasm and decided he really was cut out for teaching. By April, three other teachers and one administrator had joined the Tuesday conversations. This format caught on—and that was the start of something powerful for this middle school.

By the end of the year, faculty members from grades 6 through 8 were talking about how helpful it would be to have regular time built into the schedule to do exactly what Mary and Parker had started. They weren't looking for boring meetings where they tried to cover too much, listened to administrivia, or babbled on and on about one problem without ever coming up with a plan. Instead, the teachers wanted time to discuss crucial classroom issues, share materials and ideas, and reflect on their students' progress.

The following year, a schedule was designed that allowed small teams to have these conversations regularly. People now have two different teams to meet with on alternate weeks. One is a grade-level team that shares the same students; the other is a department team that teaches similar subject matter. All teams protect the integrity of the discussions and respect each person's time.

Wagner Middle School's process is based on appreciative inquiry conversations, a fundamentally different approach to collaboration. Appreciative inquiry addresses crucial issues by having participants share success stories and then use those stories to develop clear action plans and commitments. Because Wagner Middle School's teachers see the big difference their hard work has made, they are highly motivated to keep this process going. They still get tired from working so hard, but they no longer feel burned out.

Using this format, team meetings are now game changers. Meeting results are so practical that instruction is better the very next day. Teams make sure their meetings have four major components:

1. A topic that everyone genuinely cares about and wants to be involved in.
2. An environment where every person's contributions are valued.
3. An action plan that people see as useful by the end of every meeting.
4. Feedback that shows whether their plan works.

These meetings energize and empower people. They answer the questions, why am I in this meeting, and why should I care?

Activity 3. Meeting Protocol Reflection

1. How well do your current meeting protocols apply the four components mentioned above?
2. What improvements do you want to see in your meeting structure?

Defining Protocols and Roles

Let's look at how Wagner Middle School designed its journey of embedding a more productive and strengths-based collaboration process into its meeting structure.

Relaunching the Process

The leadership team decided to upgrade the meeting structure by giving teachers a strong voice in redesigning their protocols. The team accomplished this by developing a two-track problem-solving process: one track for working on common Tier 1 classroom concerns during regular grade-level or department team meetings, and the second track for addressing more serious Tiers 2 and 3 academic and social-emotional problems with peer coaches (see Figure 2.2).

The team track, shown on the left side of the figure, responds to general classroom needs affecting groups of Tier 1 students. This is the rule of thumb: If every classroom teacher cannot relate to the concern, it is not an appropriate topic for a team meeting. Concerns like students handing in sloppy or incomplete work, having poor inferencing skills, being unable to follow through on directions, or displaying weak memory skills are examples of legitimate team topics because every person on the team can probably name three or four students who need support in these areas. These topics lend themselves to strategies that can be embedded into daily Tier 1 classroom instruction.

The second track, shown on the right side of the figure, refers to problem solving related to specific student cases that a coach and a teacher or group of teachers work on together. These Tiers 2 and 3 concerns tend to be less common or more intense than those addressed by the team track. When a teacher chooses to enter an individual student into the Tier 2 and 3 process, there are two possible entry points: (1) Either go directly to a coach or (2) gather background information before seeing the coach by interviewing the student and his or her parents. The sequence of these two steps should fit the needs of the teacher and the case.

During the first coaching conversation, the teacher and coach design a starter plan that addresses the student's need by building on current strengths. Sometimes this is all that is needed to solve the problem. If this does the trick, the coach dismisses the case and celebrates the teacher's success.

FIGURE 2.2
The Problem-Solving Process Flowchart

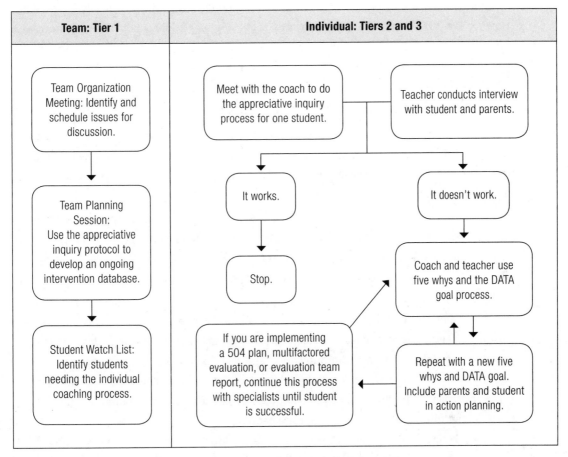

Team: Tier 1	Individual: Tiers 2 and 3
Team Organization Meeting: Identify and schedule issues for discussion.	Meet with the coach to do the appreciative inquiry process for one student. / Teacher conducts interview with student and parents.
Team Planning Session: Use the appreciative inquiry protocol to develop an ongoing intervention database.	It works. / It doesn't work.
Student Watch List: Identify students needing the individual coaching process.	Stop. / Coach and teacher use five whys and the DATA goal process. / If you are implementing a 504 plan, multifactored evaluation, or evaluation team report, continue this process with specialists until student is successful. / Repeat with a new five whys and DATA goal. Include parents and student in action planning.

If the starter plan solves only part of the problem or does not result in enough student growth, the teacher and coach proceed to the five whys part of the process. In this step, a deeper analysis of the root causes is done before a new action plan is designed. Sometimes the coach and teacher may decide to involve the family in the design right away, and sometimes they decide to try a few action plans on their own before involving the family in a student support team. Again, the type of case is what determines how quickly the student support meeting happens.

If the family and faculty have tried the student support team meetings several times and the growth is still minimal, there is probably enough evidence to support a request for additional testing by an expert. The results of this testing are often helpful in determining the next action plan, and occasionally will also include the addition of special services to the plan. If special education services are recommended, this plan gets folded into the continuation of the five whys and student support team steps. It does not replace it or end the process.

You will find many protocols for conducting productive meetings in *Teacher Teamwork: How Do We Make It Work?* (Searle & Swartz, 2015). Wagner Middle School chose to start with establishing roles and responsibilities, developing timed agendas, and using consistent protocols to keep each meeting's conversations positive and focused.

Creating Roles and Responsibilities

To get every meeting started on the right foot, each member of the team assumes a specific role. This makes things go more smoothly, especially when the coordinator keeps the team focused and the timekeeper keeps discussions moving at a good pace. Here are the specific role descriptions used:

- **Coordinator:** Build respect within the team, and ensure that discussions stay focused and detailed. Balance talk so each person has an equal chance to contribute.
- **Analyzer:** Promote clear and specific action plans and ask clarifying questions as stories and ideas for interventions, accommodations, and progress monitoring are discussed.
- **Timekeeper:** Ensure that the entire agenda is completed and no time is wasted, have meetings start and end on time, and see that time limits on the agendas are honored.
- **Recorder:** Facilitate communication and use chart paper or a projector so the team can look for patterns of what works as ideas are shared. This visual display makes it easier to develop goals and action plans. Distribute summary notes of the meeting within 24 hours to the appropriate people.
- **Summarizer:** Review progress and refocus efforts when discussions veer off course. Help team members hear their own conversation points by frequently paraphrasing what is said.

The team's 35-minute organization meeting identifies three key issues that teachers see as critical, clarifies the topics, and establishes schedules for team discussions for the next two months. Teams hold this organization meeting once a quarter

Team: Tier 1 Organization Meeting

Once roles are assigned and norms are agreed on, each team uses this three-step format:

1. Identify the top three Tier 1 concerns.
2. Pinpoint missing skills and decide how to monitor student growth.

3.   Develop a schedule for the next quarter of team meetings.

Let's take a closer look at the 6th grade team organization meeting at Wagner Middle School. There are six members on the team: John, the English teacher; Parker, the math teacher; Sharonda, the social studies teacher; Julia, the science teacher; Ramon, an intervention specialist; and Janelle, who tutors students in reading and math. This team meets every Wednesday during second period. Every other week is devoted to team problem solving using the appreciative inquiry process. Alternate weeks are used to work on a variety of team tasks. Here are the three steps they use to organize their meetings at the beginning of each quarter.

Identify the Top Three Tier 1 Concerns

For this meeting, John agrees to take the role of coordinator, Parker chooses to be the summarizer, Ramon and Janelle share the job of analyzer, and Julia agrees to be the recorder. As timekeeper, Sharonda gets out her phone so she can use her timer to keep the team moving forward on their timed agenda.

John starts by asking everyone to identify three crucial classroom concerns that they know affect a group of Tier 1 students in each classroom. Without conferring with one another, the teachers write down on sticky notes the top three student issues they want to discuss at upcoming grade-level meetings. The team agrees to select a balance of behavior and academic topics as the year progresses. Sharonda reminds the team that they have six minutes to complete this activity.

Here are Parker's three most pressing concerns:

- Students' inability to follow steps in a process.
- The lack of respect that many students show for one another.
- Students not checking their work for accuracy before handing it in.

Some of the items on Janelle's list are similar:

- Students who can't draw a logical conclusion from their work.
- The drama constantly being stirred up on social media and continued in the hallways.
- The lack of motivation to keep working when the work is hard.

The entire team's sticky notes are then sorted by similar concerns and ranked by urgency and importance. Over the next quarter, the team plans to develop action plans for the top three problems. Parker, the summarizer, makes sure the entire team agrees on the issues before moving to the next part of the meeting.

You can see a team using this process in Activity 4.

Activity 4. Organization Meeting: Tier 1 Concerns

Video 2.1. Organization Meeting: Tier 1 Concerns: https://bcove.video/34AHS6M

Video 2.1 shows middle school teachers generating their list of Tier 1 classroom concerns that negatively affect groups of students on their team. As you watch the meeting, notice the following:

1. How do team members come to consensus on the three top concerns?
2. Which issue discussed is outside this team's circle of influence?
3. How does assigning roles to each member affect this meeting?

Reflection questions:

1. What effect did the time limit of six minutes have on the team?
2. How long would the process of coming up with three top concerns take at your school?
3. Would this process relieve teacher stress at your school? Why or why not?

Pinpoint Missing Skills and Decide How to Monitor Student Growth

The next 20 to 25 minutes of the team's organization meeting is spent getting consensus on how members define and plan to assess the three selected topics. They accomplish this by answering three questions:

1. Exactly what do you see and hear that makes you think this is a problem?
2. What is the missing skill that will help make this problem go away?
3. How will we measure student growth in this area?

The top priority the 6th grade team selects is students handing in incomplete work. Julia records this as the first general issue on Form A, the Organization Meeting Form, under the column "Specific Concern" (see p. 24).

Parker sees the problem of incomplete work as papers with lots of careless mistakes. Sharonda describes it as papers that are partially completed. Janelle thinks it means missing homework assignments, and Ramon sees the problem as students giving answers without showing the process or steps involved.

The group has no trouble seeing how miscommunication and frustration are bound to occur if they do not clarify the exact result they are going for. After a bit of discussion, they decide that the change they want to see during their first four-week plan is "students checking their work for accuracy and completeness before submitting it." Now they need to turn the wording of this problem into a specific skill they want to see more of. The strength charts can help them do this quickly and efficiently. (See Appendix A for the four charts mentioned below—on motivation [p. 161]; self-monitoring [p. 168]; organization [p. 162]; and problem solving [p. 164].)

> Ramon: As I look at the motivation and self-monitoring charts, I see many possibilities on both, but I'm not crazy about any of them.
>
> Julia: On the organization chart it states, "I have daily routines and procedures that help me reduce stress and find things easily and fast." That appeals to me.
>
> John: On the problem solving chart it says, "I use models, rubrics, and checklists to self-assess my work." How about that one?

Everyone cheers, and Julia records John's idea on Form A, under the column heading "Meeting Focus." This becomes the focus skill for their next team meeting, where they will design an action plan for teaching students to use a variety of tools to help them double-check work for both accuracy and completeness.

In the discussion that follows, the team also decides on a plan for assessing student progress. This will be recorded on Form A under the column heading "Criteria for Measuring Growth."

> Sharonda: I think the best way to track growth is to have students keep their own daily chart showing how many completed papers they turned in and how many they turned in with five or fewer errors. This will provide baseline data the first week; we can then gather the weekly data for our team report. After we design our four-week action plan, we'll see if the number of completed assignments, including homework and classwork, and papers with fewer than five errors improves each week.
>
> Ramon: Recording every paper for every student every day sounds like a lot of recordkeeping. What do you think about having each teacher select four key students to track? Our team data can be based on that sample group.
>
> Everyone loves the idea.

Parker thinks about the saying, "That which gets measured gets done." He knows that when he checks the effectiveness of what he is doing, he is more likely to adjust his plans when the results are less than he hoped for. He also knows his team is counting on each team member to follow through and report back on how well the plan works, so he is less likely to let this plan fall to number 99 on his hit parade of things to do. He is fully committed to progress monitoring his students. He does have a question, though: Which students should he and his team monitor?

Once a team develops an action plan, each teacher typically monitors four Tier 1 students who need the identified skill. It is wise not to choose the most severe students for this Tier 1 monitoring. Tiers 2 and 3 students will benefit from this plan but will probably need more help than the Tier 1 plan provides. In Parker's math team, few teachers share the same set of

Form A. Organization Meeting Form

General Issue	Specific Concern	Meeting Focus (Skill we want to see more of; see strength charts)	Criteria for Measuring Growth	Start Plan	Stop Plan
Students who hand in work that is incomplete	Getting students to check their work for accuracy and completeness before submitting it	Teach students to use models, rubrics, and checklists to self-assess their work for both accuracy and completeness	Number of homework and classwork papers turned in complete (all questions answered and all steps shown, if appropriate) with five or fewer errors	9/18	10/16
Students who do not understand how to draw a conclusion (inference) based upon evidence				10/16	11/13
Students who give up when work is hard, lack of perseverance				11/13	12/11

students; in his 6th grade team, however, they do teach the same group but in different subjects. So is it better to pick the same students when possible, or should every teacher pick different students to monitor?

Either way works. No overlap provides a larger sample of students. Overlap allows teachers to compare a given student's response in different environments. There are advantages both ways.

What *is* important is that teachers agree on consistent monitoring procedures. This aligns the plan and further clarifies the type of instruction needed to achieve the four-week goal. The Wagner Middle School 6th grade team's agreement for collecting data on the number of assignments turned in complete and with five or fewer errors is clearly stated on Form A.

Within 35 minutes, the team identified the three most urgent concerns facing the team, clarified each topic for their future team meetings, and determined how they will monitor the progress of their students. The team is now ready to schedule the start and stop dates for the next three action plan implementations. As you can see on Form A on page 24, the team decided to work on "students turning in work that is incomplete" from September 18 to October 16. They plan to work on "students who do not understand how to draw a conclusion (inference) based on evidence" from October 16 to November 13, and they will work on "students who give up when work is hard, lack of perseverance" from November 13 to December 11. Because they have pre-planned their topics and criteria for monitoring for the next 12 weeks, their meetings are more likely to be efficient and data driven.

To see a video example of this part of the organization meeting, go to Activity 5.

Activity 5. Organization Meeting: Clarifying Concerns

Video 2.2. Organization Meeting: Clarifying Concerns: https://bcove.video/3a8YeET

Watch the team clarify target skills in Video 2.2. As you watch, notice the following:

1. How and why team members use the strength charts.
2. How they make their work data driven.

Reflection questions:

1. What is the purpose of the strength charts?
2. What do you think would have happened if team members had no access to these charts?
3. What does the process of deciding on the criteria for progress monitoring achieve?
4. Do you agree with tracking the progress of only a small sampling of students? Why or why not?

Schedule Action Planning Meetings

This type of meeting planning addresses one of the most frequent complaints we hear from teachers: "We start things and come up with good plans, but we seldom follow up on the plans to make sure they worked." Preplanned meetings with built-in timed agendas and assessments keep teacher stress levels down. Having the topics and timed agendas in advance saves precious time because people come prepared to dig right in.

Activity 6. Clarifying Concerns: Your Turn

Try your hand at clarifying concerns and connecting them with skills students may need to work on, as well as finding ways to monitor progress of those skills, using the blank version of Form A (see p. 27). You will see that five concerns are listed: that students are unorganized, unmotivated, disruptive, failing math, and unable to apply phonics. You may want to use the strength charts in Appendix A (pp. 154 –170) to identify specific missing skills.

Even though the general concern you find on the first strength chart you look at may be helpful, you will find that concerns fit several skills on many charts. As a team, your job is to select the one or two subskills that provide the most viable starting place. Working on too many things at once results in being effective with nothing.

After you have completed this activity, check your answers against the Activity 6 answer key (p. 151) at the end of this book.

About a week after the organization meeting, the team is ready to develop a Tier 1 plan for their first issue. They use a meeting protocol based on appreciative inquiry conversations to produce a positive action plan every time they meet. No more "discuss everything and do nothing" meetings for them.

The Meeting Protocol

Research shows that when people focus on positive talk, they tend to be more open-minded and optimistic, and they use better coping skills. Negative talk tends to magnify problems and make people feel needy or anticipate the worst (Mayo Clinic, 2018). That's why the appreciative inquiry process starts every meeting with a quick, positive connect activity and ends with a commitment to a measurable goal and specific action plan.

Form A. Organization Meeting Form: Your Turn

General Issue	Specific Concern	Meeting Focus (Skill we want to see more of; see strength charts)	Criteria for Measuring Growth	Start Plan	Stop Plan
Unorganized					
Not motivated					
Disrupts the class					
Failing math					
Cannot apply phonics					

The conversation guide for team meetings in Form B features the following six-step protocol for strengths-based problem solving.

Step 1. Connect

John knows that Ramon hates touchy-feely activities, so he carefully explains the connect step:

John: The connect step builds relationships, trust, and respect; it starts each meeting on a positive note. This two-minute positive talk boosts our flow of dopamine, the neurotransmitter in the brain that opens our minds to seeing options and being more creative.

Ramon's eyes flash to the ceiling, but his little grin indicates that he will go along with the process.

John: I'll start by asking every person to respond to a lead-in question. Because this team has only six people, there's no need to break the group into subgroups like we do in our department meetings. Here's your question: What profession would you have chosen if education had not been an option for you? Sharonda, how long does each person have to answer?

Sharonda: About 20 seconds to stay within the two-minute time frame on our conversation guide and give all six of us an opportunity to talk.

Julia: I would have chosen to be an airline pilot.

Janelle: What made you choose that, Julia?

Lead-in questions can produce laughter and fun or lead indirectly to the topic under discussion. Analyzers try to elicit details, feelings, or insights when answers are too brief. These questions always establish positive energy and encourage people to share interesting thoughts and feelings without having to become too personal. Here are sample questions borrowed from corporate leaders who use this process regularly:

- What is the best thing that has happened to you this week?
- What is the most important thing you have learned as a result of your job?
- What would you like to accomplish as a result of being part of this team?
- What is the most satisfying part of your job?
- If you could talk to one historical figure, who would you choose and why?
- What character would you like to play if you could be cast in a favorite movie? Explain.
- What slogan could you live by?
- What is the funniest thing a staff member (or student or parent) has ever said to you?
- If you could choose only one vacation destination, what would it be and why?

Form B. Team Conversation Guide

Date:			
2 min.	**Connect:** What do you appreciate about this team? What do you like best about being a teacher?	This starts the conversation on a positive note. (Examples of other questions: What are your best accomplishments this week? Who inspired you to become a teacher? What would you like to be known for? What was your funniest school experience? What is your favorite book, movie, place to visit, etc?)	
2 min.	**Review the concern/focus:** What outcome would be most beneficial for these students?	Concern	Meeting focus (this is set during the organization meeting and reviewed here to focus the stories)
9 min.	**Share success stories:** Ask the teachers to describe a time when they helped struggling students become very successful at this skill. Be very specific about the following: 1. What the student did 2. What you did that helped 3. What the parents did 4. What the other students did	Team's specific success stories	How does this strategy change student thinking? (It may help to refer to charts.)
6 min.	**Establish a DATA goal:** If we apply what we know to this situation, what could happen in four weeks?	**Do:** If we teach students to _____ **Achieve:** We will see this outcome: _____ **Time:** In __ weeks **Assessment of growth:** They will improve by ___ percent	

Action plan for the next four weeks

9 min.	**Design an action plan:** What ideas from the story are the best fit for this group of students?	Ways teachers will support	Suggestions for parents	What students do for themselves

7 min.	**Commit to an action:** What small step will each teacher act on tomorrow to move the plan forward? What will each person do to support the group? How will each teacher monitor student growth?	Teacher name	Tomorrow I will start by . . .	How will I support the team?	Progress monitoring

- Who was instrumental in your decision to choose this career?
- If you could choose one age to be for the rest of your life, what would it be and why would you choose it?

Activity 7. Team Planning Meeting: Connect

Video 2.3. Team Planning Meeting: Connect: https://bcove.video/2Vs08Lv

As you watch Video 2.3, observe how this 7th grade team generates positive energy and builds camaraderie.

Reflection questions:

1. What effect does this activity have on this team?
2. List three connect questions that would suit your team.
3. What value do you see in using this step for your team meetings?

Coordinators choose connect questions that best match their teams' personalities and situations. If the question generates positive energy, the content of the question doesn't really matter.

Step 2. Review the Concern/Focus

Once creative juices are flowing, the team is ready to review the concern and meeting focus generated during the organization meeting. Like most teams, the Wagner Middle School 6th grade teachers are willing to invest energy in problems they view as clear, real, and important. They lose enthusiasm and commitment when the problem is vague or insignificant. Because every meeting they hold is based on a previously identified learning opportunity that affects multiple students, the Wagner team meetings generate practical plans that are easily accepted by team members.

For example, one concern teachers had was fighting and bullying, so team members chose a meeting focus from the strength charts of "teaching students strategies for creating a culture of kindness and support." When the problem targeted was student reluctance to put thoughts and steps down on paper, the meeting focus selected was "teaching successful ways for students to become more confident in their ability to express themselves in writing."

These clear focus statements generated at the organization meetings are quickly reviewed and inserted into the conversation guide so the team can move quickly to Step 3.

Step 3. Share Success Stories

Successes shared create a sense of hopefulness in place of any previous frustration that might have occurred. The story part of the conversation serves as a discovery process that uncovers the team's collective know-how about what works. Each person on the team responds to the focus issue with a positive, personal story that helps the team see new possibilities. Because team stories are real-life experiences or observations, the strategies described have credibility and intensify the belief that the final plan will be realistic and practical. These strategies are recorded on the left side of the story ideas T-chart shown in Figure 2.3.

Each time a team member offers a success story, the team tries to view each scenario through the student's eyes to figure out the reason the strategy was successful. They record these insights on the right side of the T-chart. This results in a much richer and more helpful list than brainstorming ideas only.

> John: Now we will each share a story about a time when you were successful helping students move from a habit of handing in incomplete work to a habit of being careful and dependable. Your success stories may be school based but can also come from outside school settings. A story about how students performed as a member of the basketball team, on the playground, or as a cast member in a play is often more insightful than simply looking at daily classroom responses. What's our time frame this time, Sharonda?
>
> Sharonda: We have nine minutes to generate both stories and reasons why these strategies are successful.
>
> Julia: I'll type the ideas and reasons why they work on a T-chart on my computer today. I'm linked with a projector so everyone can see what I'm typing. You will have the added advantage of receiving an electronic copy right after the meeting. Hopefully, this visual will help us pick up on patterns of what makes students successful. It will also make the selection and consolidation of ideas easier during the action plan design step.
>
> Parker: I'll get us started. One-to-one tutoring is what helped Lorraine move in just four weeks from an average of 62 percent to 93 percent in terms of turning in more complete and accurate work. It worked like a charm with her.
>
> Janelle: What was it about your one-to-one tutoring with Lorraine that made such a difference? Was it the cueing, type of questioning, or kind of feedback that was the real magic?
>
> Parker: I used the "I do, we do, you do" idea of gradual release to first model what I expected of her. Then I had her practice using a rubric before I faded my support.
>
> Janelle: So under the "story ideas" on the left side of the T-chart, we want to say that modeling helps them visualize what to do and the gradual release provides practice with corrective feedback?
>
> Parker: That sounds right to me.

As personal experiences or things learned from others come to light, analyzers ask, "What made that strategy work?" This brings up valuable insights into how the original strategy must be implemented in order to have a significant effect.

FIGURE 2.3

Story Ideas T-Chart from the 6th Grade Team

Story Ideas for Helping Students Establish Efficient Routines and Procedures	Effect on Student Thinking (Strength charts may help here)
1. I modeled and helped Sophia set up a folder system for each day of the week. She placed things to do on Monday in the Monday folder. The "to do" items were sometimes incomplete work or new assignments. If she didn't finish the work on Monday, she moved it to the Tuesday folder so she wouldn't forget it. Sometimes notes with reminders to do things at home went in the folder as well. For instance, "I need to talk to the librarian" went into the Thursday folder and "Wash my soccer uniform" went into the Wednesday folder so she would be ready for her Thursday game.	• This reminder system is used for everything, not just for schoolwork. • Sophia sees a practical reason for doing this because it's not just for schoolwork.
2. I gave Miguel sticky notes at the beginning of class. He wrote down at least 9 or 10 things he needed to do before class ended, some small and some bigger. Very big tasks got broken up into smaller pieces because he needs lots of breaks. This process took about three minutes to do after he got used to it. His list looked like this: 1. Get out my book, paper, and pencil. 2. Take notes. 3. Compare my notes with Jordon's or Asia's notes. 4. Do my science lab with notes. 5. Take a 1-minute break. 6. Finish the science lab with notes. 7. Take a 1-minute break. 8. Write my conclusion. 9. Put my science lab notes in my binder. As he did each thing, he could wad the sticky note up and toss it basketball style into the trashcan. He taught this organization strategy to a few other kids because he liked it, and they wanted to throw paper wads, too.	• Breaking large tasks into smaller pieces helps Miguel relieve stress. • Adding a bit of fun with breaks and throwing paper wads is appealing. • It also acts like a 3-D checklist. It always feels good to mark off your progress. • The element of fun is always inviting. • Having Miguel teach the strategy reinforces the steps and emphasizes his new strength rather than making him feel weird or different.

Story Ideas for Helping Students Establish Efficient Routines and Procedures	Effect on Student Thinking (Strength charts may help here)
3. With Annette, I used a treasure hunt game to keep her motivation up. Every morning, she and three friends would set a timer for 90 seconds. I would have three things on a card that they would need for class, like the worksheet from yesterday, their math lab notes, and a pencil. If they all found all three things in 90 seconds, they won the race. There were no prizes or penalties. It was a game they found enjoyable, and they began to see that if they had a system for where they put things, they could win every day. If they did the jam and run method (where they jam their papers into their backpacks to run to their next class), I would get the point for the day.	• Playing with friends as a team helped Annette because they would give one another ideas for improvement and because they played against the timer and not against one another. • The timer helped them feel a sense of urgency to design an efficient system for organizing their things. • The fact that I didn't tell them how to organize or double-check their progress gave them a sense of ownership and kept them tweaking their system for improvements.
4. Jamal rarely could find any of his mistakes, so I started coding the type of mistake in the margins of his paper. For example, if he had an addition error, I would put a blue plus sign in the left margin. His job was to find the error and circle it in pencil. He gave himself a point for every error he identified correctly. Once he found it, he could get an extra point for fixing the error, and he could ask for help if he wanted to.	• This made Jamal more aware of the kind of errors he was making. • He was more willing to fix them because the task was not so overwhelming. I started by only marking one or two types of errors, and as he improved, we expanded. • Keeping his own data gave him ownership. I didn't care if it was perfectly accurate. I just wanted him to learn to identify errors and know it was OK to learn from them. He did!

If team members mention something like, "I sent the student to the tutoring center or to special ed," Janelle knows that these are programs, people, or places—not strategies. She asks for details about what happened in that setting to get back to a focus on strategies.

Asking exactly what was done and what effect the strategy had on a student's thinking opens up a spectrum of ideas beyond the one successful strategy offered. The team looks for *patterns* of things that work rather than just for the single technique mentioned. Here are a few questions that Janelle and Ramon use to draw out specifics and find out why certain strategies can be so effective:

- Exactly what changed in the student's way of thinking as a result of what happened in this story?
- Why did that lesson appeal to the students? Was it the visuals, the hands-on approach, the students' choices or the students' inclusion in designing the plan, the level of background knowledge they had, modeling, discussion, peer work, self-monitoring, chunking into smaller steps, lack of time pressure?

- What caused the new response? Was it a different routine or procedure, a different practice strategy, physical environment changes, scheduling adjustments, new ways of giving feedback and celebrating successes, different visuals, graphic organizers, technology, other resources?
- How did that feel for students and adults?
- Could you give an example of what that looked like in your classroom?
- What resources did you use for that lesson?
- How did you fade your accommodations to promote more student independence?

If discussions start to generate punishments or ways to bribe students into compliance, Ramon is quick to redirect the conversation to more helpful alternatives. As the summarizer, Parker periodically recaps the key ideas shared. This not only shows respect for everyone's contributions but also highlights the team's progress toward the new plan of action. By restating suggestions in different words, he makes sure the team sees any new patterns for learning that may have surfaced in the discussion.

Figure 2.3 shows what the 6th grade team's storytelling session came up with. Notice that the analysis of the effect on student thinking is what enables the team to see strategies through the eyes of students and expands team options when it comes to designing the action plan.

Because the team approaches the storytelling conversations with enthusiasm, out-of-the-box thinking, and willingness to contribute powerful ideas, the conversations create excitement and a commitment to new levels of student achievement and behavior, as well as feelings of hopefulness for the teachers. Their degree of success rests on the quality of the stories, the insights as to why the strategies worked, and the way these story ideas will be woven into practical and bold designs for change. Watch the video clip in Activity 8 to see a team telling their success stories.

Activity 8. Team Planning Meeting: Focus and Success Stories

Video 2.4. Team Planning Meeting: Focus and Success Stories: https://bcove.video/3eiu9Ga

As you view Video 2.4, imagine yourself as the recorder. Why is capturing strategies and observations on chart paper (see Figure 2.4) helpful for the team members?

FIGURE 2.4
Charting Team Stories

Specific ideas from stories	How does this benefit students?

Reflection questions:

1. What did each member do to facilitate this conversation?
2. How will putting the effect each strategy has on students on the chart help the team?

Step 4: Establish a DATA Goal

Once the team's stories generate a compelling list of options, team members develop a clear learning target to guide their design. This target takes the form of a measurable DATA goal (see Figure 2.5) describing both the hypothesis for change and the progress monitoring part of the plan.

FIGURE 2.5
DATA Goal

Hypothesis:	**D:** If we teach students to **do**_____ ,
	A: then students will **achieve** _____ .
Monitoring:	**T:** What **time frame** will we use for implementation and assessment?
	A: How will we **assess** student growth?

Sharonda: We can take six minutes to write this DATA goal.

John: I think we can do that because the idea of doing things differently always starts with the statement, "If we teach students to do . . .", whereas the achievement part of the goal completes the if/then hypothesis. Julia, would you read what we already have from the organization meeting minutes?

Julia: The skill we chose from the problem solving chart was this: "Teach students to use models, rubrics, and checklists to turn in work that has been checked for both accuracy and completeness." So this becomes the "if" part of the statement if we still like it.

The team agrees it still fits.

John: Originally our concern was the lack of complete and accurate assignments being handed in, so that should be the "then" part of the hypothesis.

Everyone agrees.

Parker: Let's try this DATA goal on for size: "If we teach students to use models, rubrics, and checklists to self-assess their work for both accuracy and completeness, then they will be able to complete and hand in more quality assignments."

The team likes the statement, so this hypothesis becomes the guiding statement for developing the action plan. They think that four weeks will be fine for seeing results from their action plan. Teachers will continue using these effective strategies even when the team's focus moves to another concern.

Julia: We already established a way to monitor the progress of student growth during the organization meeting, but sometimes the original idea doesn't fit once we start putting together a plan. Our original idea was to have the students tally the number of homework and classwork papers turned in that are complete—all questions answered and all steps shown, if appropriate—and tally papers having five or fewer errors. Someone suggested that our rate of completed assignments should show at least a 20 percent improvement for us to consider our plan successful. Is that still what we want?

Everyone agrees.

Sharonda: We have agreement, and it only took four minutes. Now we move on to designing the action plan. We have nine minutes for that, and I can give you the extra two minutes we just saved if we need it.

To personalize the progress monitoring, each student records his or her own starting score and target to reach within the four-week period. Chelsea, who is currently turning in three out of five assignments, sets a target of four out of five in four weeks. Sophia, who is handing in no assignments right now, agreed to a target of three out of five completed assignments submitted by week four, even though this is more than a 20 percent increase. Teachers can adjust targets for individual students if the team agrees on what makes sense. Remember that this is a Tier 1 plan that can be used with the entire class, but the students selected for data reporting to the team will be four Tier 1 students who need to improve this skill as opposed to the extreme cases.

Teams sometimes use a percentage of growth for the group, and sometimes they set individual student goals. Whichever method makes the most sense to the team is the one to choose.

The DATA goal will now become the guiding statement as the team designs an action plan that will help students meet their target goals.

Step 5. Design an Action Plan

After writing the DATA goal, Parker starts by reviewing the key points generated by the stories.

Parker: We know that the following ideas play to both our teacher and student strengths:

1. Building in an element of fun with games and beating your own best score works, especially if teams of kids are encouraged to help one another.
2. Having students model strategies and teach one another makes learning stick through verbalization.
3. Applications outside of school life make using these skills seem real.
4. Checklists, rubrics, and sticky notes are always winners because visuals help kids see connections and increase learning.
5. Teaching students to break big tasks down into smaller chunks relieves stress.
6. Letting students make choices and decisions helps them own the process.

We want to base our plan on these six insights.

John: Now we're ready to select and expand on our story strategies and the insights Parker just listed to develop a plan that matches our DATA goal. While designing the action plan, keep in mind that a balance of accommodations and interventions is what works best for promoting independence and enduring change.

Accommodations. *Accommodations* are supports put in place by adults that facilitate student learning. Examples are reading text to them, shortening assignments, chunking material, and modeling and practicing correct procedures. Because accommodations are teacher controlled, when this type of support is withdrawn, students are often not able to maintain quality work or improved behavior independently. Accommodations are helpful in the initial stages, but their overuse often results in learned helplessness.

Interventions. *Interventions* are strategies intentionally designed to promote student independence. Direct instruction followed by guided practice and feedback ("I do, we do, you do") sets the stage for the gradual release of responsibility. The phasing out of teacher-led activities and phasing in of student-led planning, choosing, applying, and evaluating make student success more likely to endure when direct teacher support is no longer available. Examples of interventions are having students learn to chunk their own work, asking students to self-monitor their behavior so they can reflect and adjust where needed, explaining which strategies work for them and which do not, and having students learn a variety of study skills and apply them in unfamiliar situations.

Activity 9. Accommodations and Interventions Sorting Activity

Sort the eight ideas listed into three categories: accommodations, interventions, neither.

1. Have the student set a goal for how much work he or she can accomplish in five minutes and measure his or her improvement over two weeks.

2. Give preferential seating in math class so you can give the student regular feedback.

3. Cut student assignments in half and only grade the completed portion.

4. Provide the student with one-to-one instruction.

5. Have the student divide long assignments into smaller pieces to avoid becoming overwhelmed.

6. Have a partner check the student's math fact accuracy three times a week using flashcards.

7. Have the student attend Title l reading class.

8. Have the student identify body signals that might alert him or her to a possible anxiety attack and have him or her choose a self-calming activity that would help.

Check your answers against the Activity 9 answer key on page 152.

Activity 10. Team Planning Meeting: Design

Video 2.5. Team Planning Meeting: Design: https://bcove.video/2RxH5yf

As you watch Video 2.5, notice how the story ideas helped the teachers come up with new learning possibilities based on what typically worked in the past.

Reflection questions:

1. What happened to the plan as the teachers widened their thinking to home and student activities?

2. What was the most powerful idea they came up with? Explain.

3. List two other strategies that would fit into these patterns of student and teacher strengths if this is their DATA goal:

If we teach our students to develop a personalized organization plan, they will remember to bring and be able to find the materials they need for class.

Within four weeks, students will increase their time and accuracy for having and finding three things within two minutes by at least 50 percent.

The team in the video decided to begin by modeling and discussing a variety of organization strategies so students could design their own organization plan. The teachers also decided to assess progress by using the treasure hunt idea. Some students needed a lot more support than others, so the team eventually developed a way to scaffold the plan at four different levels in four different ways.

Figure 2.6 shows the four basic adjustment categories for teaching a difficult skill. You can adjust the level of difficulty, the level of support, the size of the task or time allotted, and the type of feedback. Because students don't all need the same amount of assistance, the goal is to get them to independence and mastery quickly without frustrating them. Any student can be plugged into the exact type and level of support they need to begin with and then move to the right on the chart toward greater independence as they improve.

This design enables teachers to create personalized plans for students. If a student gets frustrated, a teacher can move him or her to the left, toward greater teacher assistance. Some students could start with a minimum of assistance for size and feedback but with moderate assistance for difficulty and support.

An ounce of action is worth a ton of theory. The longer you wait to begin a plan, the weaker the chances of strong implementation. Now it's time for team members to decide what they will start doing right away.

Step 6: Commit to an Action

Now that the team has its action plan, it is time for each member to commit to a specific starting place. How many times has your school or team decided to implement a new program only to drop the ball on the follow-through? That won't happen here.

John: We know it's easy to agree a plan is worthwhile, but we take things to an entirely different level when we give voice to what we are each willing to do to make it happen. Now it's time for me to ask every member to commit to a small change they will implement immediately. This commitment can be as simple as reading an article or observing someone else doing one strategy. It can be as involved as starting the class using one of the ideas in the action plan. Specific commitments will not only launch our action plan quickly but also provide the beginning point of discussion for our next meeting on this plan.

Julia: I'll start. I plan to create a checklist of things students can look for before they hand in their math assignments. I will limit it to just four or five things so the checklist doesn't seem like another assignment.

Ramon: Would you like help on that? We could work on it together and share it with the team.

FIGURE 2.6

Adjustment Options: Helping Students Get Organized

	Maximum Help	Moderate Help	Minimum Help	Independent
Difficulty	Teacher models and leads the organizing practice sessions.	Teacher sets up categories, and student partners file papers.	The student sets up categories, checks with partner, and decides how to file. Teacher checks work.	Student sets up categories, files his or her own papers, and then checks with teacher.
Support	Small-group practices are held before the large-group lesson.	Partners practice together.	Partners set up categories, but each student files papers on his or her own.	Student decides categories and files own papers.
Size	Student starts with two categories: today's and tomorrow's papers. 5 minutes to file	Student sets up three categories: today, tomorrow, and tools I need. 4 minutes to file	Student sets up four categories: today, tomorrow, the next day, and tools I need. 3 minutes to file	Student sets up six categories: all five weekdays plus tools I need. Add outside-of-school tasks. 2 minutes to file
Feedback	Track and chart how many seconds student takes to find his or her work over a four-week period. (Teacher guides this.) Teacher asks what went right and suggests ideas for improvement. Daily	Chart seconds student needs over a four-week period. Partners discuss what went well and choose an idea for improvement from strategy list. Every 2 days	Chart seconds student needs over a four-week period. Individual student explains what worked well and what didn't. Partners decide what improvements to make. Every 3 days	Chart seconds student needs over a four-week period. Student self-assesses what worked and suggests ideas for improvement. Weekly

Parker: I'll work with my class tomorrow on creating a rubric for planning presentations. We're about to start math presentations. I think using a rubric before I get started will help, especially if the kids help me design it.

Sharonda: The four kids I have in mind are all a bit overwhelmed by all the work they have to do, so I would like to start by using the sticky note strategy John uses with Miguel. Could I come over to your class and watch you do this with him tomorrow?

John: Certainly, I think Miguel would be honored to teach you his technique. He may even agree to come to your class and work with your four students to get them started. My starting point will be to create a recording sheet for my students so they can keep track of how many completed assignments they hand in and how many of their assignments have five or fewer errors. I'm sure each of you will need a sheet like that to collect our team data, so I'll share it and count this as my team support idea as well.

Janelle: My starting place will be to look for checklist and rubric ideas on the internet to see what fits middle school math and reading. I can share that information and count it as my team support idea as well.

John: Does anyone need to adjust the way we decided to collect data to fit their own situation? No? We do need to decide how many data points to collect, however.

Ramon: We should use this week to get baseline data on our four students and then have the students chart their own data five days a week on the form John is developing. We can then use their recording sheets to compile our data once a week for the Team Progress Monitoring Form [see Form C].

The commitment step completes the six-step protocol for team problem-solving meetings. From this point, each team member monitors the progress of four students who are representative of the Tier 1 group targeted to use the intervention plan. The instructional group can either be the entire class or a subgroup needing the skill.

Each teacher uses the agreed-on method of measuring growth by comparing the baseline scores of the four students (collected right after the organization meeting) with the students' weekly improvement scores.

After two weeks, the team holds a quick check-in to report results they have observed in their classrooms. It is too soon to make final judgments about the plan's effectiveness because lasting changes take longer than two weeks to appear, but the team may decide to tweak or add to the strategies. After four weeks, the team discusses the student data to figure out if the new plan needs adjustment or expansion or if it's time to switch the focus to another issue. This is what data-driven decision making is all about—using daily classroom information to drive practical action plans that affect daily classroom instruction.

Activity 11. Team Planning Meeting: Commit

Video 2.6. Team Planning Meeting: Commit: https://bcove.video/3chKyZB

As you watch Video 2.6, notice how the commit portion of the meeting affects the team's energy.

Reflection questions:

1. What will the team discuss in two weeks?
2. Will their plan be a data-driven decision-making conversation at that point? Why or why not?

Form C. Team Progress Monitoring Form

What Is Being Measured	How the Team Will Collect Data

Student Name	Baseline	Week 1	Week 2	Week 3	Week 4	Total Growth
A.						
B.						
C.						
D.						

Activity 12. Determining Strengths and Needs: Calvin's Case

Now consider the following scenario:

> Rebecca is a 3rd grade teacher who is having a hard time getting her class to work in groups. One of the main problems is a boy named Calvin. None of the kids want him in their group. Calvin is an attractive-looking boy who has a difficult time fitting in. He is very bright and continually shouts out before anyone else has a chance to answer. He jumps into conversations with gusto to insert his point of view, and when he speaks to people, he makes good points but gets right into their face as he talks. Because his hygiene is sometimes poor, kids shy away from sitting anywhere close to him. He is sad about the fact that he has no friends, but he seems totally unaware of why this is happening.

What strength chart would you use to identify strengths and needs for Calvin (see Appendix A)? What three suggestions for an action plan would you give to Rebecca to get her started?

- Strengths Calvin has that we can build on:
- Skills that would help him gain friends:
- Suggestions you could give to Rebecca that would help Calvin:

Tips from the Field: In Their Own Words

This completes the six steps for addressing student concerns at the Tier 1 or classroom level. In this "Tips from the Field" section, which appears in Chapters 2 through 6, practitioners who have been successful with this approach offer helpful advice. Here, they share tips that will help you fine-tune the plan for your team meetings:

- "The team organization meeting is repeated every nine weeks in our school. Sometimes we work on the same topic we selected for the first four weeks at a more intense level, but most of the time we switch our focus to new concerns that surface. This allows us to grow our database of strong interventions for teaching specific academic and social-emotional skills."
- "Our school identifies one academic and two behavior concerns for team meetings for the first and fourth quarters and then one behavior and two academic concerns for the second and third quarters. This pattern helps us balance our choices and focuses us on the specific skills our students need before the state tests."
- "We learned that designing strategies *before* we clarify the exact change in student behaviors or skill levels we want to see causes our planning process to be less focused and sometimes unproductive."

- "Our team takes notes on a computer attached to a projector so everyone can see the notes as they are developed. At the end of the meeting, we just e-mail the notes and the topic for the next meeting to everyone."

- "Putting together people who have regular, common planning time is the criterion for our teams rather than what subject they teach or which students they share. The structure of the team is not an issue because the concerns that teams tackle generally cut across departments and grade levels. For example, academic issues can be poor reading comprehension, the inability to write complete sentences, or having a limited vocabulary. Behavioral concerns are frequently topics like having difficulty paying attention, having a poor memory, being unable to follow directions, or being disruptive in class. Social-emotional issues might be the failure to make and keep friends, an inability to deal with stress, or starting and promoting conflict and drama. Each of these problems looks a bit different as students get older or go to different classes, but they tend to be universal difficulties that most teachers see regularly no matter where they teach."

- "If you are a specialist who serves multiple grade levels, you may need to submit your concerns and success stories electronically because scheduling may not allow you to attend all team meetings. SurveyMonkey, Zoom, or Google Forms are easy formats for communicating with teams you cannot see face to face."

In a Nutshell

This process saved Parker from leaving the profession. Once he connected to a supportive team, he saw how powerful and rewarding education could be.

How many Parkers do you have in your building? They may be teachers who are new to the profession or new to your system, or experienced teachers struggling to meet the needs of a changing population and changing times. We all need support, encouragement, and help with upgrading our skills to keep our stress levels to a minimum.

This simple procedure launched a major shift in the way the Wagner School faculty thought about and addressed problems. Topics that teachers had previously griped about in the teachers' lounge became topics for a proactive way of supporting staff and students. In the next chapter, we explore ways to help parents and students embrace a partnership with teachers by using the same positive approach for problem solving.

3

Nothing About Us Without Us: Student and Parent Conversations

Wagner Middle School has problem-solving coaches trained and ready to go, but for two years the faculty has taken minimal advantage of this valuable resource. Unclear expectations and unanswered questions caused these busy educators to take a wait-and-see attitude. Questions like "Is this going to create more work for me with little payoff?" or "Whose job is it to get this ball rolling, and how do I access this new service when I need it?" have yet to be clearly addressed.

Last month, the multitiered systems of support (MTSS) coach invited teachers to request a conference with her if they wanted her support in finding ways to help individual students. Parker is worried about several students in his 6th grade math class, but he is especially concerned about Cassie. Her potential seems high when she is answering questions orally, but her performance is consistently low when she has to work things out for herself, no matter how many times he explains the problem.

Cassie used to come to class prepared and willing to do her work. She tried hard at first, but that seems to be changing. She's consistently making mistakes on all but the simplest of math problems. Any problem that requires two or more steps throws her into an "I can't do this" attitude. It wouldn't be such a big deal if she would ask for help, but her modus operandi is to guess and keep going. As a result, she has failed almost every quiz in the last five weeks, and her once pleasant attitude is looking more like sadness and hopelessness. Parker decides to schedule the coaching session and give this new procedure a try.

Parker is delighted with the fact that Daphne, the MTSS coach, agrees to see him almost immediately; he doesn't have to wait for weeks or prove that he's already done 39 interventions before he can access this process. He is also surprised that he doesn't have to fill out a pound of paper in order to get help. That's a big change from the protocol in his other school. Here's what their initial conversation sounds like:

> Daphne: Parker, how well do you know Cassie in terms of who she is outside of class—her interests, dreams, learning preferences, and strengths?
>
> Parker: You know, when I try to think of specific things other than her math skills and attitude in class, I guess I really don't know much about her at all.
>
> Daphne: Here's a quick Student Interview Guide [see Form D] that you can use to get to know her better before we meet next Tuesday. This problem-solving process is always more productive when you can figure out what makes the student tick. The interview takes about 15 minutes and uses nonthreatening, open-ended questions that most students can answer easily.
>
> Parker: That sounds like it would be worth doing. Thanks!

Form D shows the six steps that Parker will use. It focuses on making connections, sharing success stories, reflecting on what helps, identifying strengths, clarifying needed supports, and committing to next steps. Daphne cautions Parker to not get into his agenda about fixing Cassie's math problem at this stage, as it's too early for a problem-solving session. She also offers to assist in the interview, but Parker feels confident that he can manage the process on his own.

To his surprise, Cassie is reluctant to give him anything more than the most cursory of answers to his questions. Parker feels frustrated when he sees Daphne the next day.

> Parker: I don't know why she wouldn't open up. Mostly I heard "I don't know" and "I can't think of anything" as she looked at the table or her feet. I only asked the first two questions because it didn't feel like the conversation was helping. Maybe those questions weren't the right ones for Cassie.
>
> Daphne: I'm sorry that happened to you, Parker. You were wise not to push her. That would have been counterproductive. Because this is our first year in the process, I really should give teachers more information on ways to make students comfortable. There are three other teachers about to interview students. Maybe we can all meet at lunch and go over some dos and don'ts that avoid the problem you faced yesterday.

During the group lunch, Daphne shares her own experience as a beginning teacher. She wishes she had asked more questions and listened more intently to what students had to say daily. Her busy schedule sometimes made her forget about building relationships.

Form D. Student Interview Guide

Interviewer:	Student:	Date:	
Purpose	Get to know the student's strengths and thoughts		
1. Connect: Tell me something you've done that you are proud of.			
2. Share success stories: Think of a time when you had to do something very hard and you were successful. What is special about you that helped you do that?			
3. Reflect: What things do teachers do that help you learn?			
4. Imagine: If you got the best student award this year, what would it be and what would you have done to get it? (Reference a strength chart here.)	Strengths the student identifies from the chart	What they want to get better at	
5. Design an action plan: What could we do together to make the award happen?	What would you like me to do to support you?	What would you like your parents to do to help?	What could you do?
6. Commit to an action plan: What will we both do to start this plan? What small step will we each take? When should we meet again?	Tomorrow the teacher will		Tomorrow I will

Preparing for the Student Interview

When we ask students what they think about participating in these interviews, they are forthcoming about why they clam up. Students say that when they are invited to an interview, it triggers the same feelings as being sent to the office. Even if they are sure they haven't done anything wrong, the initial feeling of anxiety is there because they don't know what to expect.

Here are some tips from students that should pave the way for more productive discussions:

- **Students aren't always sure you really care about them as people, even when you do.** Doing little things like calling them by name when you see them in the hallway or expressing appreciation for small things they do well goes a long way toward building positive relationships. Education consultant Rick Smith (2004) suggests using the 2-by-10 strategy for the most reluctant students. This involves having two-minute conversations for 10 consecutive days on a topic the student wants to talk about. This can get off to a rocky start if the student doesn't want to talk, but don't give up and don't press the student for conversation.

- **Students are sometimes anxious or suspicious about why you are asking these personal questions.** You can put them at ease by explaining your purpose and asking their permission before you start. This might sound like, "Good morning, Cassie. I'm trying to get to know my students better so I can be more helpful. I already know about things you do in class, but I can't know what you like or how you think without having a conversation with you. You could really help me out by answering a few questions. Is that OK with you?"

- **Students are sometimes concerned that they won't give the correct answers.** Early in the conversation, explain to the student that the questions you will ask are the kind you *can't* get wrong. Point out that everyone has their own way of seeing things and that you are interested in hearing how they think and feel.

- **Students sometimes want to answer, but the teacher rushes them so they lose their words or can't think.** Firing one question after another or offering your own answers when there's silence has a negative effect on communication. Remember, your job is to listen and learn and do as little talking as possible. Brief affirmations, clarifying statements, and wait time are helpful; adding too much of your point of view is not.

- **Students don't always believe that teachers sincerely want to listen to their ideas,** whether it's because of the look on the teacher's face or the teacher's attitude. People are more apt to believe your tone and body language than your words.

Body Language Matters

Here are some tips from educators about maintaining a welcoming tone and friendly body language:

- Sitting side by side or knee to knee for the interview sends a friendlier signal than placing yourself behind your desk. The library may feel like a friendlier environment than the office or classroom.
- Have you ever had someone smile at you, but their smile doesn't reach their eyes? Trust goes out the window when that happens. Leaning forward with your body, staying relaxed, making comfortable eye contact, and smiling communicate that you're listening and interested.
- Your tone of voice also projects either an inviting attitude or says you are all about getting this over with. Judgmental looks or tones can shut the conversation down fast. Your tone, words, and body language must communicate interest and respect for students' thoughts and feelings. Videoing yourself during a student interview can be an eye-opening experience that enables you to check out how you are coming across.

Because Parker got off to a bad start with Cassie the first time he tried the interview process, he thinks that inviting Daphne to the next interview will be helpful. Daphne suggests that they tag-team. She will start off by modeling a way of putting a student at ease, and then Parker can jump in with questions when it feels right. You can see the interviews in Activity 13.

Activity 13. Student Interview: Cassie's Case

Refer to the strength chart on resilience and flexibility (Appendix A, p. 167) as you read this interview. As you read the dialogue, list specific things Parker and Daphne do that

1. Relieve Cassie's stress.
2. Encourage her to think more deeply about her strengths and needs.
3. Uncover useful information for future planning.

Daphne: Hi, Cassie. I'm Daphne Stiller. My job is helping teachers figure out the best ways to support their students. Mr. West invited me to join your conversation because he thought he may have made you nervous the first time you talked. Do you mind if I sit in this time?

Cassie: No, it's OK. I was nervous.

Parker [smiling]: Sorry about that. Holding student interviews is new to me. I guess I was feeling anxious, and I passed it on to you.

Cassie: That's OK. I always get nervous around teachers.

Parker: Maybe we can change that by just talking to each other more often. Is it OK with you if we start that same conversation again? I'm really interested in getting to know you better, and I think the questions on this sheet are helpful. The nice part is that there are no wrong answers, so neither one of us can make a mistake. Do I have your permission to try again?

Cassie: Sure, but I might not be able to think of an answer.

Parker: No problem. Mrs. Stiller is here to help both of us if we get stuck, and we can skip some questions if we want.

Cassie: All right. [Cassie's body posture relaxes a little.]

Parker: The last time we were together, I asked you to think of something you've done that you're proud of. Did anything come to mind?

Daphne: It doesn't have to be something that happened at school. Just think of anything you've done that makes you smile inside.

Cassie [pausing, then shyly smiling]: Last week I made four goals for my soccer team. My family went crazy, and that made me smile.

Parker: I'll bet it did! You can't do something like that without a lot of hard work. Tell me what's so special about you that you got good enough to pull off something so hard.

Cassie: My coach helped me.

Daphne: And what did you do that made that possible?

Cassie: Lots of practice. Sometimes I wanted to quit because for a long time it seemed like I couldn't do anything right.

Daphne: But obviously you're not a quitter because here you are with four goals. When you felt like quitting, how did you talk yourself out of it, and what made you hang in there?

Cassie: My dad and coach kept pushing me.

Daphne: But you could have refused to try again. Some kids do quit even when adults insist. What makes you different from those kids?

Cassie: I don't know. [Long silence.] I wanted to make my dad happy, and after I practiced over and over, I got better. My coach kept showing me over and over and drawing sketches on paper to help me remember what to do. Finally, it worked.

Daphne: So it took a long time, but when you saw yourself getting better, you kept trying. I heard you say that you set a goal to make your dad proud. Setting goals works for a lot of people. The other thing I heard was that you need to see teachers and coaches model, and it helps to see the steps on paper. That helps you remember what to do. Is that correct? Those are helpful pieces of information about what works for you. Take a look at this strength chart on resilience and flexibility and see how many of these things you already do for yourself.

Cassie: I see the one on setting goals and the one on making pictures in my head. I do that in soccer, but I don't always do that at school. I *do* look for people to help me when I'm stuck at home. Sometimes at school I don't ask, though.

Parker: Do you see something in the chart that you'd like to get better at?

Cassie: Maybe the one about asking for help would be good.

Parker: I love it when students know when to ask for help. It makes my job so much easier. What can we do together to make that happen?

Cassie: I don't know.

Daphne: Students often need different types of help. Some just need a quick check-in to see if they're on the right track before doing an entire paper wrong. Others need to have the steps or directions clarified because they don't understand what to do. Which of these do you generally need?

Cassie: Sometimes both, but I hate to be the only one to keep asking for help. It makes me feel stupid.

Parker: If I give you a card that has a blue side for check-in times and a red side for "I'm stuck and don't understand," you could put it on your desk. Depending on the side that shows, I'll be able to tell what you need. In fact, I could do that for everyone because it would help lots of kids feel more confident about asking for help.

Cassie: I'd feel better about using that method.

Parker: Why don't we start that tomorrow? I'd appreciate it if you'd use your card at least once a day for the first week. Are you willing to do that?

Cassie: I guess so. That seems like a lot.

Parker: It will just help us get used to the system, and then we can decide where to go from there. I really want you to feel comfortable asking for help. It's the mark of a strong and confident person not to wait until someone has to ask you if you need help. That's a great goal to set for yourself, and I want to help you with it.

Reflection questions:

1. Is there anything you would word or ask differently during the interview?
2. Where might this interview process fit into your school day?

What They Learned from the Interview

This interview enabled Cassie to identify her strengths; she also became aware of the fact that she doesn't always apply those strengths at school. This is a great step toward helping her build on what she already knows works for her outside of school.

Cassie left the interview feeling heard and appreciated. Parker felt both encouraged and concerned. He was encouraged by the new goal and the impression that Cassie wouldn't shut down the next time he wanted to talk with her, but he was frustrated by the fact that they didn't come up with a solution to the math issue. They hadn't even talked about math.

Daphne reminded Parker that the purpose of the student interview is to strengthen the student–teacher relationship and gather helpful background knowledge needed to support Cassie. Keeping the entire focus on Cassie's thoughts and feelings is what made the interview successful. Discussing the math problem at the initial interview would have diminished the positive feelings. Daphne assured him that the insights about Cassie's strengths, interests, and goals would be helpful in designing a solid math plan later on, and once the relationship is solid, it will be easy to hold conversations that focus on specific math skills.

Activity 14 shows another example of a student interview. This time we will look at a younger student, a 5-year-old entering kindergarten.

Activity 14. Student Interview: McKinley's Case

Video 3.1. Student Interview: McKinley's Case: https://bcove.video/2K1FooC

As you watch Video 3.1 of this student interview, notice the following things:

1. What was the teacher's purpose for this interview?
2. How did the teacher give the student both voice and choice?
3. How did the teacher make it comfortable for McKinley to talk about herself?

Reflection question:

1. What question would you add and what question would you eliminate to make the questions fit your own students?

Preparing for the Parent Interview

After congratulating Parker on his stellar performance during the student interview, Daphne suggests tapping one more valuable source of background information—Cassie's parents. She explains that the same cautions and tips she suggested for student interviews apply when interviewing parents. It's always about establishing relationships based on developing trust and mutual respect through using good listening skills.

Researchers (Hoover-Dempsey et al., 2005) identified three key factors that determined whether parents or caregivers decide to become involved in their children's education.

How welcome parents feel about coming to school. Imagine how you would feel as a parent if a teacher called to say that your son or daughter was doing well in school or that they just wanted to meet you to get to know your child better. Be prepared for them to sound pleasantly surprised. Parents are not accustomed to parent-teacher conferences that focus on identifying the strengths and interests of their children. That is the focus of the parent interviews in this book.

Whether parents believe their help will have a positive effect on their child. Parents' perception of what involvement requires of them either moves them forward or scares them silly. If every night parents and children get into an all-out war over homework, a caring parent has to wonder how much damage this kind of "help" is doing. When parents struggle with reading or writing themselves, it's understandable that helping their child may not yield many positive results.

It is also important to consider how reasonable our home assistance requests are. A single mother with two jobs and three children is hard-pressed just to keep everyone fed, happy, and healthy. Asking for 30 minutes of uninterrupted homework help for each child may be more of a dream than a realistic goal. We need to ask for things that parents believe are within their capabilities, time constraints, and knowledge level if we want them to make and keep commitments. When parents feel that the tasks are reasonable and that what they say is valued, they have an easier time seeing themselves as partners in the education of their children.

Whether parents believe it is their role to help. Parents are the experts on how their children feel and think. Asking them to fill you in on their child's background knowledge, likes, interests, and dreams is a role parents feel comfortable with. This is a perfect way to start building the relationship between home and school.

The Parent Interview Checklist

It's important to communicate how much you value the parents' partnership in supporting their child's learning. Here is a checklist for conducting a positive parent interview:

1. Clarify that the purpose of this interview is to gather helpful background information on their child. Let parents know that you see them as the prime experts in this area.
2. Start the interview by asking questions that encourage parents to describe their child's positive traits and experiences.
3. Continue with questions that help parents reveal how their child learns best and what strategies work well for honing both academic and social and emotional skills.
4. If parents focus on weaknesses or punishments they use, turn the conversation back to their child's strengths, interests, and learning styles.
5. Ask parents what goals they have for their child.

6. Ask for their ideas on how you can work together to support those goals.

7. Save your personal goals and concerns about their child for another time, unless they match the parent's goals and concerns.

8. Close by making commitments to each other for next steps and schedule a follow-up meeting or phone call.

We know that parents' beliefs and behaviors have a huge influence on their child's success in school. Creating a safe and welcoming environment for both students and their parents is a key to success.

The Parent Interview Guide

Parker feels as though his successful interview with Cassie will give him the confidence and skills he needs to interview her parents. He is reassured by the fact that the questions in the Parent Interview Guide (see Form E) reflect many of the questions in the student guide.

The Parent Interview Guide suggests interview questions, but it is in no way meant to be prescriptive. Many other questions may fit as well or better. Here are a few alternatives:

1. What do you remember as your child's best day (or best day at school)?

2. What is a favorite wish your child has?

3. If you could tell teachers one thing that would help your child learn better, what would it be?

4. What do teachers do that sometimes interferes with the way your child learns?

5. At the end of the year, what do you hope your child says about this year? What is the story you hope he or she would tell?

6. What are your fears or concerns about your child this school year?

7. Is there anything else you can tell me about your child?

8. Is there a question you wish I'd ask about your child?

9. How often and when would you like me to be in touch with you?

This interview is designed to be 100 percent positive and supportive. Its purpose is to develop a safe working relationship with the family; the teacher should bring up no problems or complaints at this stage. The mantra is "listen, encourage, and listen some more."

Activity 15 describes Parker's interview with Cassie's parents. As you read the dialogue, you will notice that some of the questions are straight from the guide, some are paraphrases of those questions, and others just flow naturally from the discussion.

Form E. Parent Interview Guide

Date:	Parents' Names:	Student:	Grade:
Purpose	To get to know the student better through the parents' eyes		
1. Connect: Tell me something your child accomplished that you are very proud of. What strengths made that happen?			
2. Share success stories: Think of a time when your child was frustrated but worked through it.			
3. Discuss supports: What are things you do to support learning and positive behavior for your child? What actions cause frustrations?			
4. Imagine: If this were the best school year ever for your child, what one change would make that happen? Would your child agree with this?			
5. Design an action plan: What things can we do together to make that kind of school year happen for your child?	What the parent could do	What the teacher could do	What the child could do
6. Commit to an action: What small step can we start with tomorrow?			
7. Communicate: What would be the best way for us to stay on the same page? When can we talk again?			

Activity 15. Parent Interview: FaceTiming with Cassie's Mother

Parker scheduled a room in the library to meet Cassie's parents, but he ended up holding a FaceTime conference because of family transportation and scheduling problems. He remembered to introduce the process by clarifying the purpose and asking for help in getting to know Cassie through her parents' eyes.

As you read through the interview, consider the following:

1. How do you think Mrs. Ramirez felt after this interview?
2. What good listening strategies did Parker use?
3. What helpful information was uncovered that Parker would not have learned without this parent interview?
4. How did Parker get a commitment for immediate action from Mrs. Ramirez?

Parker: Thank you for taking the time to talk with me. I'm talking to the parents of my students so I can learn ways to make math class more effective for them. I'd like to start by asking you to tell me one thing about your daughter that you're especially proud of.

Mrs. Ramirez: Well, Cassie is a wonderful big sister. I can always count on her to look out for Nina. As you know, 5-year-olds can be cranky and annoying, but Cassie is so patient, even when things get a little rocky.

Parker: As a parent of three children myself, I'd be ecstatic if my older kids treated the younger one like that. Kindness and patience are important traits for successful people. So when Cassie does become frustrated with something, as we all do at times, how does she get herself through those situations?

Mrs. Ramirez: She *does* get frustrated, especially with homework. When it gets too much for her, she either puts her head down and cries or goes into zoned-out mode. Once that happens, you might as well just stop because she totally shuts down.

Parker: Can you think of a time when you knew she was on the verge of tears but was able to get through the frustration and go forward? It doesn't have to be a homework example. Any frustrating time that turned into a success story is good.

Mrs. Ramirez: Yes, she often wants to give up on soccer, but she bounces back more frequently now. Her coach is good about giving the girls enough encouragement to keep them from getting discouraged.

Parker: What does he do exactly?

Mrs. Ramirez: One thing he says all the time is, "That was a tough play. How do you feel about that?" Then he waits for an answer; sometimes for a long time. Then he asks Cassie what she did right and what would work better next time. Most times, Cassie can't give him an answer, so he just smiles, walks away, and says he'll be back later for her idea. At first, the fact that he wouldn't help her come up with the answer really upset her. She complained like crazy, so we talked to him about it. He explained to Cassie and to us that to be a good player, she has to learn to figure out at least one way to fix her own problem before asking for his thoughts. Not that her ideas are always good ones, but he makes her at least try to solve things for herself first. Then he offers additional ideas and has her try again. The team had a tough time accepting this way of coaching at first, but now they're used to it and it seems to work with all the kids. They're a really good team now.

Parker: Thank you for that information. This coach sounds like someone who knows how to help kids grow. Do you think I could use his technique in math with Cassie? I know lots of students are having a tough time now that we're doing more complicated problems.

Mrs. Ramirez: That makes sense to me. She shuts down when she's doing math just like she used to in soccer. Another thing that Cassie likes about this coach is the way he explains his ideas by drawing things out on paper. She has a notebook full of his drawings, and she goes over and over that information before practices and games.

Parker: Good for her. That shows a real dedication to learning. Those ideas are worth their weight in gold to me. I can't thank you enough! Is there anything else you do at home that helps Cassie?

Mrs. Ramirez: I can't think of anything except that when we stay calm, things go better. Once we lose it, she does, too, and nothing good happens after that.

Parker: If you could choose one thing that would make Cassie's year more productive, what would that be?

Mrs. Ramirez: She has a hard time remembering what she's supposed to do. I have to repeat directions five or six times, and even then she frequently comes back and asks what I said or just lets things slide. It's like things just don't stick with her, and it doesn't matter if it's people's names, spelling words, or how to set the table. She's always had this problem.

Parker: Yes, I see that tendency in math class, too. I have a chart [see the strength chart on memory in Appendix A, p. 160] that lists skills students need to make their memories strong. I'll send it home so you can take a look at it. I'd be interested in knowing which strengths you see in Cassie and which item from the chart you think we should work on.

Reflection question:

1. What other questions would have improved this interview?

What They Learned from the Strength Chart

After Mrs. Ramirez looked at the memory strength chart, she wrote back to Parker that she noted three of Cassie's strengths: that she recognizes important ideas, asks for breaks when she's working on something, and asks for help when she needs it. She felt that the one thing that would most help Cassie remember is testing herself on material. Parker responded that he thought that having Cassie repeat steps for directions and tasks *before* beginning them would be a good starting place for school and home support. He also mentioned that he would contact a colleague who might be able to suggest some helpful memory strategies. He promised to get back to her by Wednesday of next week.

Parker was glad he had taken the opportunity to get input from Mrs. Ramirez. It changed the way he thought about what Cassie needed to succeed in math class.

Activity 16. Parent Interview

Video 3.2. Parent Interview: https://bcove.video/3eiOnQh

As you watch Video 3.2 of this parent interview, notice the following things:

1. How did the parent seem to change as the interview progressed? What caused these changes?
2. What information did the teacher uncover that will be helpful in the classroom?

Reflection questions:

1. What do you see as the pros and cons of having this kind of interview with parents?
2. Think of two students you want to build a strong relationship with. How do you think the parent and student interviews would affect these two students?

Tips from the Field: In Their Own Words

Educators share their thoughts about the parent interview process:

- "Parent involvement needs to go beyond just rewarding or punishing their children for being compliant and working hard at school. Parents can work on social-emotional and executive function skills that benefit children with both home and school tasks."
- "When we interviewed parents using this process, they said they felt honored, valued, and listened to. Even parents who had no problems with the old way of conferencing described this technique as a breath of fresh air."

- "We suggest that the teacher do minimal note taking during these interviews. Sometimes students and parents wonder what you are recording and why. This distracts them from the conversation."
- "If parents take the conversation in the direction of 'what's wrong with my child?' or just vent, don't let that go on long. Assure them that you hear what they're saying and that identifying strengths and interests is the first step in working with them to solve problems. Get back to talking about their child's strengths and interests as quickly as possible."
- "Many teachers in our schools use this Parent Interview Guide during parent conferences. Parents enjoy the conversation, and teachers find this discussion more helpful than simply giving them a progress report."

In a Nutshell

Research shows that school–home communication is greatly increased through personalized, positive contact between teachers and parents. When teachers convey good news and show real interest in hearing what parents have to say, the relationship between home and school improves.

Student and parent interviews are designed to build rapport and promote a solid partnership for supporting social, emotional, and academic growth for students. These conversations need to feel safe, useful, comfortable, and playful. The student and parent should always leave feeling that the faculty cares deeply about them and is willing to flex and support as needed to help the student learn and grow.

It is important to go into these interviews not assuming things; these are opportunities to learn everything you can about what makes the student tick. We all want students to become independent and responsible; when teachers and parents work together, it's easier to develop the "I can" beliefs that help students see themselves as capable. This attitude makes students more likely to persist in the face of frustration and advocate for themselves when they need help.

If we want students to take an active role in their own learning, it is imperative that we intentionally include them in setting their own goals, designing their own action plans, and monitoring their own growth. Providing students with the opportunity to have open discussions with teachers and parents about their successes and struggles builds the trust and skills needed for learning independence and responsibility.

In the next chapter, we will look at coaching conferences that take the information gleaned from the parent and student interviews and apply it to designing new learning possibilities.

4

The First Meeting with a Coach

Even the most efficient protocol in the world cannot effectively solve problems if nobody uses it. We see this pattern of passive omission in many schools. It's not the lack of caring but, rather, the lack of a systemic plan for launching the process that causes the problem. People wait for someone else to take the first step to get help for a student who begins to struggle. Sometimes this waiting game ends up allowing a student to fail who could have passed the course or met the benchmark for performance—*if* he or she had only been given an early intervention.

To avoid this syndrome, we suggest creating a student watch list at the beginning of every school year. Teams of teachers then update that list every nine weeks. These lists of high-priority students are given to the team of school coaches, so every student on the list has a double set of eyes monitoring his or her progress and designing intervention plans.

Creating the Student Watch List

To avoid the "wait and see if someone else does it" pattern of the past, the Wagner faculty starts a triage process to identify students who are likely to need extra support. This is based on a combination of suggestions from last year's teachers and what current classroom teachers and specialists are seeing. Here's how this process works.

Each grade-level and department team devotes six minutes of their first team meeting to generating this list of students for coaches and teachers to check on regularly. Each teacher identifies his or her top three students in need of support. These are often not the students who already have a support system in place. Watch list students are those who are likely to fall behind because of academic, social-emotional, or executive function needs that may or may not currently be addressed by other services but are worrisome to the classroom teachers.

Coaches distribute these cases among themselves and quickly touch base with these students' teachers to decide whether they need to schedule a coaching conference to codevelop an intervention plan or whether the case calls for a weekly check-in with the student and teacher to see if they are making progress. Each coach becomes a talking partner who supports teachers with ideas and resources. Coaches also serve as a second set of eyes on students who need extra support.

Here's how one 6th grade team meeting proceeded:

John (Coordinator): Good morning. Today we have a quick but important task to accomplish. First, we will each think of three students who might slip through the cracks if not given immediate attention. Write each student's name and a short description of what worries you on a separate sticky note for each student. I'm going to ask you not to confer with one another as you write. We will then prioritize this list of students and give it to our coaches, who will follow up with you in the next week or so to see what type of support you need. How long do we have for this, Sharonda?

Sharonda: Six minutes total. Two minutes to write and four minutes to sort and prioritize our list for the coaches.

The analyzers, Janelle and Ramon, help the team compile and rank the names in order of urgency. The time limit helps the team resist the urge to go into detailed descriptions and discussions of students' problems. Parker summarizes and checks for team consensus on the list. Julia, the recorder, compiles the watch list, which is given to the team of coaches. To see a team working through this step, watch the video clip in Activity 17.

Activity 17. Student Watch List

Video 4.1. Student Watch List: https://bcove.video/2V9LOly

As you watch Video 4.1, notice how the team's use of roles helps facilitate the meeting.

Reflection questions:

1. What protocols do your teams currently use to make meetings efficient and effective (e.g., roles, timed agendas, distribution of notes, procedures for consensus)?
2. How do your teachers ensure that students don't get off to a rocky start at the beginning of the school year?
3. How long would it take your team to identify a watch list like this?
4. Would submitting three student names and concerns electronically work better at your school? Who would this list go to for action?
5. Who supports you in coming up with classroom intervention plans for students who do not qualify for specialized services?

Once a watch list is established, the coaches begin to touch base with the teachers who teach these students. At Wagner Middle School, Cassie was one of the students the 6th grade team put on the watch list.

Setting Up the Coaching Conversations

Now that Parker knows Cassie and her family better, he's ready to set up a coaching conversation with Daphne. During this 35-minute session, Parker and the coach follow the same appreciative inquiry format that was used during his team's problem-solving meeting. This time, however, his focus is strictly on Cassie instead of on a group of students. Nevertheless, he knows he can certainly apply whatever action plan he comes up with to other students who might need similar supports.

Who Attends

Because Parker initiated this problem-solving process, he gets to call most of the shots. The teacher who requests the conference may choose to meet individually with a coach or may invite other faculty members. Often fine and applied arts teachers add a helpful perspective. Faculty providing counseling or tutoring services can also offer valuable insights. Sometimes other teachers of the student in question who don't experience the same problems contribute valuable information about what works. In Cassie's case, the soccer coach may be the best resource person to invite, if the parents give permission. Parker decides to start the process by himself and add others later if he needs them.

When to Request a Coaching Conference

Anytime a teacher is at a loss about what to do to support a student, a coaching conference is helpful. It's wise not to wait until students are in over their heads. Many research studies show that early interventions are most effective for reducing long-term risk, especially when the interventions empower families as well as faculty (Bailey et al., 2005).

Establishing the Coaching Protocol

The appreciative inquiry approach is built on the premise that you get more of what you pay attention to. That's why the coach asks the teacher to think of stories about what is going right to fix what is not going well. The more the teacher knows about what the student already responds well to, the easier it is to build a plan that gets more of what the teacher wants to see.

The purpose of the coaching conversation is to build an action plan based on the approaches, adjustments, and environments that work best for a specific student. The six-step process shown in the Initial Coaching Conversation Guide (see Form F) suggests questions to use, but coaches need to listen carefully and adjust those questions to bring out the most productive ideas during these sessions.

The coach starts the discussion with a connecting question designed to generate upbeat responses. Questions like "You spend a lot of time planning lessons and creating a great work environment for your students. What functions best in your classroom?" or "Who inspired you to do great work when you were a kid?" spark creative juices and place us on the road to seeing the glass half full.

If a coach chooses to use a student-focused question, it should bring the student's strengths to light as opposed to the student's weaknesses. Things like "What would Judy's best friend see as her finest trait?" or "What dreams do you think Judy has for her future?" are helpful questions. Questions that ask about deficits like "What changes does Judy need to make?" or "What concerns you most about Judy?" take the conversation down the "glass half empty" rabbit hole. Negative thinking saps people's ability to stay energized and motivated and limits their vision for a positive outcome. That's why a positive connecting question is essential.

Coaching Scenario: Starting the Meeting

Because Daphne knew that Parker's interview experiences had gone well, she started the session by asking this connecting question: "What's the best thing you learned about holding student and parent interviews?" Parker smiled and started rattling off how he felt and what he learned. Here's part of that conversation:

Form F. Initial Coaching Conversation Guide

Date:	Coach:	Teacher:	Student:	Grade:

Purpose	To design new learning opportunities based on this student's strengths and needs		
2 min.	**Connect:** Tell me what you like best about being a teacher. What do you appreciate about this student?	This starts the conversation on a positive note.	
6 min.	**Review the concern/focus:** What outcome would be most beneficial for this student?	Concern in teacher's words:	What skill to teach the student (strength charts may help here):
7 min.	**Share success stories:** Ask the teacher(s) to describe a time when a student was successful learning this skill, being very specific about the following: 1. What the student did 2. What the teacher did that helped 3. What the parents did 4. What the other students did	Ideas from your stories:	How will this strategy affect student thinking (strength charts may help here)?
6 min.	**Establish a DATA goal:** If you apply what you know to this situation, what could happen in six or fewer weeks?	**Do:** If we teach _____ to _____ **Achieve:** We will see this outcome: _____. **Time:** In ___ weeks **Assessment** of growth: He/she will go from ____ to ____ .	
8 min.	**Design an action plan:** Based on the story, what ideas are the best fit for this student?	Action plan for the next four to six weeks.	

8 min. (cont.)		Things I will do:	Suggestions for parents:	Things the student will do:
6 min.	**Commit to an action:** What small step will the teacher act on tomorrow to move the plan forward? What will happen the following week? How will this skill be monitored?	What I will start tomorrow:	How I will monitor progress:	

Parker: I can't believe I have overlooked the wealth of information I could have been tapping all this time, but the best part is the subtle change in Cassie. She's happier, even though nothing has improved as far as her math goes. I picked up lots of important things from both Cassie and her mother that I believe will be helpful as we plan.

Daphne: Can you give two or three specifics?

Parker: Sure. Cassie loves soccer. There's a lot of math involved in soccer, and I can build Cassie's interests into math problems so she sees the real-life application. I was also impressed by things her coach does, like requiring the girls to try their own strategy instead of jumping in and doing their thinking for them. That is one wise dude. I'm definitely going to try that. I did hear how that idea frustrated the kids until they gained confidence in themselves, so I'll proceed with caution. Oh, and the best thing was the memory issue Cassie's mom pointed out. I guess I already knew that, but I wasn't thinking about addressing memory problems to turn her math difficulties around. By the way, thanks for modeling how to use those charts when we talked to Cassie. I've had those charts for weeks and never really looked at them. Big mistake. I did use the memory chart with her mother, and that helped us zoom right in on specifics.

The energy created by the positive start was just what Daphne was hoping for. Next, she helped Parker turn his concern to a specific skill that Cassie needs.

Daphne: When you looked at the strength chart on memory [see Appendix A, p. 160], did you target specific strengths and needs?

Parker: Yes, and I remembered your advice about choosing only one thing to work on at a time. Mrs. Ramirez went right to "test myself regularly to see if I remember." I totally agree with that, but I thought the box at the top of the second column, which talked about noticing patterns, was better suited to math.

Daphne: Actually, those two areas of memory don't sound like too much to take on because they complement each other. Let's try wording the "what to teach" statement by combining the two ideas. How about, "Teach Cassie strategies for seeing and remembering patterns and steps?"

Parker: I like that. Can we adjust that to "seeing and remembering patterns and steps in math?"

Daphne: We can, but it would limit the plan. Other teachers and the parents can apply seeing patterns and steps to many situations. Keeping it broader would make the action plan more effective. Is that OK with you? Now we need a success story from you.

Once the teacher has a clear focus on a skill, the success story is used to build the starter ideas for the design, just like it did in the team meeting.

The Success Story:
Doing More of What Works

The right questions are the heart of appreciative inquiry, but the story is the core. Success stories search for the best in both the teacher and the student; they help uncover what know-how currently exists. Check out the success story in Activity 18.

Activity 18. Success Stories: Parker's Case

As you read the story portion of this coaching conversation, look for the following:

1. How does the coach help Parker concentrate his answers on strengths and successes rather than on Cassie's deficits?
2. Watch for ways the coach draws out ideas for why a strategy works for Cassie.

Daphne: Because the new skill we've decided to focus on is about seeing and remembering patterns and steps, I want you to think of that red-letter day when Cassie was able to do that well. Although it may not have lasted the whole period, when did you see energy and enthusiasm from her? As you talk, I'll capture the highlights on chart paper. On the left, I'll list things that worked, and on the right, we'll list *why* these things work for her. That will help us see patterns in Cassie's strengths and how she thinks and learns best. We'll work on this for about nine minutes, and then we'll get to the action plan.

Parker: Energy and enthusiasm for math aren't what Cassie is about. The best I can do is tell you about the day we did a project on area. She was working with a partner to design three dog runs. Each run had to have a different shape but the same amount of area. Then they had to make a case for which design their dog would like best. Cassie dug right into that assignment.

Daphne: Perfect example. Why did that excite her?

Parker: I'm not sure. Maybe it's because she had a new puppy and just thinking about him having a run was cool. It could also be that she loves sketching and drawing, according to her mother. Her soccer coach has her draw diagrams. That's how he gets her to remember patterns for plays, come to think about it.

Daphne: So you're saying that visuals, especially ones she draws herself, could be a good memory tool for Cassie.

Parker: Yes, and working with a partner, depending on who it is, increases her enthusiasm.

Daphne: What is it about partner work that helps her?

Parker: I don't know. [Long pause.] It could be that having a partner relieves some of her stress.

Daphne: In what way?

Parker: She can ask questions or get ideas when she gets stuck. She can articulate her ideas without being embarrassed, just in case she's wrong.

Daphne: What do you think is the biggest plus for her? The chance to verbalize her thinking or the safety of not being embarrassed when she makes mistakes?

Parker: Good question. Do I have to choose? Her coach has her verbalize steps and directions to help her memory, and that works. Not looking stupid in front of your friends is a basic need for most people. I know that's a big deal, especially for Cassie, who's very shy. Let's keep both ideas on the chart.

Daphne: Absolutely. What else helps her?

Parker: The coach also makes Cassie figure out an answer to her problem before he offers help. That's something I'm going to incorporate into my teaching for everyone. My good intentions to support students too quickly may be making them too dependent on me.

In an inservice session I attended last fall, the speaker mentioned that speaking for about 10 minutes and then having students turn and talk to a partner about what should be in their notes is a good way to strengthen both memory and note-taking skills. That would work for Cassie because it's low-risk checking with a partner and oral reinforcement.

Daphne: OK, so let's look at what we have so far [see Figure 4.1].

FIGURE 4.1

Story Notes for Cassie: Seeing and Remembering Patterns and Steps

What Works for Seeing and Remembering Patterns and Steps	Why It Works
Drawing	Helps Cassie visualize what she needs to remember
Partner work	Relieves stress because she can ask questions without embarrassment Helps her articulate as she works
Time to think on her own before jumping in to help her	Helps her be less dependent
Turn and talk with a partner	Reduces stress and strengthens memory

Daphne: Did I miss anything?

Parker: That's amazing. From the story about one lesson and her soccer coach, we got all that! I see why this works. We're looking past the strategies to figure out the exact categories of things that work for Cassie. That's cool. I can already see how those four things can work in any math class, and not just for Cassie. Ryan and Megan hold back on trying strategies they aren't sure of, too.

Daphne: Now you're getting what appreciative inquiry is all about—using success stories to see what's working and then making sure you do a lot more of what works. You're a quick study, Parker. Are you ready to set a measurable DATA goal for Cassie so we can design your action plan? I want you to imagine Cassie six weeks into the future. What do you think we can expect from her if we build a plan based on these ideas?

Reflection questions:

1. How do you currently use student strengths to build intervention plans?
2. What tools can you utilize from Parker's story that would help refine your team's problem-solving process?

To see a coach holding the first part of a coaching meeting series, watch the video in Activity 19.

Activity 19. Connect and Focus: Max's Case

Video 4.2. Connect and Focus: Max's Case: https://bcove.video/3emzEDP

In this series of video segments, you'll see a coach holding the 35-minute coaching meeting with three teachers who all have the same concern about Max. Sometimes this step is done with a coach and just one teacher, as in Parker's case, and sometimes a group of teachers attend.

As you watch Video 4.2, consider the following:

1. Notice the focusing questions and paraphrasing skills used by the coach.
2. List Max's strengths and concerns identified by the teachers during this part of the discussion.

Reflection questions:

1. How did having multiple teachers at the meeting help?
2. How does narrowing the concern to one or two issues affect team problem solving?

Activity 20. Success Stories: Max's Case

Video 4.3. Success Stories: Max's Case: https://bcove.video/2REha86

Video 4.3 demonstrates the focus and success story parts of the coaching meeting. As you watch, consider the following:

1. What resonated with you in this clip?
2. What strengths did the teachers identify for Max that they could build on? (See the listing in Figure 4.2.)
3. What did the coach do to deepen this conversation?
4. Why did Rachael end the conversation by presenting an if/then statement?

FIGURE 4.2

T-Chart for Recording Success Stories and Why They Work for Max

Strategy	How It Benefits Max
Songs and chants	Rhythms help him hear patterns
Repeated practice	Builds confidence as he experiences more success
Acting out parts of a story	Helps him make connections to characters and the story
Using manipulatives	Helps him visualize what he reads and hears

Reflection questions:

1. Why is it important to consider how the strategies from the success stories benefit the student before designing the action plan?
2. Give examples of coaching skills you saw that are critical to a successful conversation.

In this video, you heard Rachael limit her talk to probing questions, clarifying statements, and summarizing the findings of the group. The kinds of questions asked and the ability to summarize important findings are key to successful coaching conversations. Coaches who jump in and try to solve things are not nearly as successful as those who are able to pull the answers from what the teachers say and highlight what they already know about the student.

As a result of looking at the success story effects, the teachers now see patterns for the types of strategies and supports Max is likely to respond to. Now it's time to project what is possible to achieve within the next four to six weeks.

In the words of Yogi Berra, "If you don't know where you're going, you may end up someplace else." Developing a clear and measurable goal is essential for ensuring that your action plan doesn't go "someplace else" or nowhere at all. Let's now look a little deeper at DATA goals, a concept we introduced in Chapter 2.

Creating a DATA Goal

The DATA goal starts with an if/then statement or hypothesis. First, we come up with what we're going to **D**o differently, which is teach the new skill the student needs. The statement always begins with the sentence starter "If we teach students to . . . " followed by the **A**chievement part of the goal, which is the change we want the student to make as a result of learning this new skill. This if/then hypothesis is built by combining the gist of the new skill from the strength chart with the original teacher concern.

For example, Cassie's inaccuracy in math is Parker's original concern, and "teaching Cassie ways to see and remember patterns" is the essence of the focus skill he identified as her greatest need. Combining these two ideas produces the hypothesis "If I teach Cassie to see and remember patterns, she will complete more problems correctly on her own." This is a well-written hypothesis for testing Parker's theory.

Parker completes the DATA goal by establishing the amount of **T**ime needed and the **A**ssessment criteria to use to predict and judge Cassie's growth. This hypothesis serves as the guiding statement for developing the action plan.

Parker wants to work on his plan for five weeks. He thinks the best way to assess Cassie's growth is to compare the average number of three-step math problems she now completes correctly to the number she completes correctly in five weeks. As he looks at his gradebook for baseline data, he sees that her current percentage of correctly completed three-step problems is zero. As he projects the target for her growth in five weeks, he believes three out of five is reasonable. Now his DATA goal sounds like this:

D: If I teach Cassie ways to see and remember patterns,

A: then she will accurately complete more math problems on her own.

T: In five weeks,

A: she will go from completing zero out of five three-step problems accurately to three out of five, without assistance.

The typical amount of time for implementation is four weeks, but this may be shortened or extended to up to six weeks if needed. If the ultimate goal cannot be accomplished in six weeks, the teacher breaks the larger goal into subgoals, as Parker did. His ideal is for Cassie to complete five out of five problems accurately, but he thinks that is too aggressive for a five-week implementation. Cassie would be devastated if Parker pushed her too hard. Challenge without frustration is the secret to success.

Looking at goals written by other people and applying a checklist for quality are good ways to become proficient at writing your own goals. Try the goal practice in Activity 21.

Activity 21. DATA Goal Practice

Use the Checklist for Quality DATA Goals (see Figure 4.3) to make recommendations on how to strengthen each of the following three goals:

Goal 1. If we teach Jill the rules, she will be able to sit still. In three weeks, she will go from distracting others an average of six times per class to zero times per class. (*Note:* Three adjustments are needed here.)

Goal 2. If we teach Senji to write good paragraphs, he will complete more research assignments. In three months, he will complete four projects. (*Note:* Four adjustments are needed here.)

Goal 3. If we allow Jerome to leave the class two minutes early, he will be able to make transitions on time. Within four weeks, he will change classes without being a disruption 80 percent of the time. (*Note:* Two adjustments are needed here.)

Analyzing the Goals

Let's now look at the three goals and see how we can improve them.

Jill's Goal

- *Adjustment 1:* Because you've probably already taught Jill the rules you want her to follow, reteaching them is unlikely to help. The **D** in the DATA goal needs to identify a new skill that Jill will learn to use independently. Sitting still may be useful in school, but success in life will take more than that.
- *Adjustment 2:* What do you *really* want for her? For her to be more sensitive to situations or others' feelings? To extend how long she pays attention? To be more engaged during class? She can be sitting still and learning nothing.
- *Adjustment 3:* Going from six disturbances per class to zero is unlikely for most children, let alone someone like Jill. You can set a reasonable benchmark for her by collecting and averaging data on five other active children who are not regular disturbers and then phasing her into that number slowly. If she can't see herself being successful, she won't stay motivated to keep trying.

FIGURE 4.3

Checklist for Quality DATA Goals

Do		What will we teach the student? (This is not what the teacher will do. It's the new skill the student will learn.)
		Is this intervention different from what we did with the student in the past that did not work?
		Is the skill found on one of the strength charts?
Achieve		Does the achievement goal address the teacher's original concern?
		Does this improvement translate beyond school to great life skills?
		Does the goal describe growth in skill for the student, not just compliance?
Time		Is the time frame for growth six weeks or less?
Assessment		Does the assessment measure the hypothesis stated as the target achievement?
		Does the assessment measure in small increments so the student can see growth weekly?
		Does the assessment include baseline data and a target for expected growth?
		Is the expected growth reasonable for the time given?

Using the self-regulation and impulse control strength chart (see Appendix A, p. 169), here is Jill's new goal: If we teach Jill to adjust her energy level to match the situation, she will be able to pay closer attention and reduce disturbances. In four weeks, she will be able to summarize what was just said in class three out of six times, and she will reduce disturbances from six per class to three.

Senji's Goal

- *Adjustment 1:* The idea of writing good paragraphs is OK, but it's much more helpful to decide *which* parts of paragraph writing Senji needs to focus on. Using the strength chart on writing (see Appendix A, p. 170) to identify what he's already good at can help you identify which subskill will be the best place to start.

- *Adjustment 2:* Completing more research assignments is a good school goal, but you can improve it by turning it into broader life skill—for example, "he will be able to clearly express his ideas in writing" or "he will be able to find and cite sources to back up his claims."

- *Adjustment 3:* As far as the timing is concerned, three months is too long. Six-week (or more frequent) check-in points are essential. If you don't see progress in four to six weeks, you need to adjust your intervention plan.

- *Adjustment 4:* Completing four projects doesn't help you to know whether Senji grew or not. You need a baseline and a projected benchmark score. For writing, it's wise to judge quality as opposed to quantity, and a rubric is always the best way to judge quality.

Using the writing strength chart, Senji's new goal now sounds like this: If we teach Senji to support ideas with facts, evidence, and examples, the quality of his research papers will improve. In five weeks, he will go from scoring 45 points on the research paper rubric to 65 points.

Jerome's Goal

- *Adjustment 1:* Although it's a helpful accommodation, allowing Jerome to leave early doesn't teach him a new skill that will eventually make him independent. Once the teachers stop giving him extra time, what will happen? A better suggestion might be "If we teach Jerome to develop and critique his own plan for transitions, then his ability to get to class on time will improve." This teaches a life skill as well as addressing the school version of the problem.

- *Adjustment 2:* Making transitions on time is a good life skill, but it doesn't match what is being measured in the assessment part of the goal. What exactly does the teacher want to see from the student? Is it being on time or not being a disturbance as he enters the class? Establishing a time limit of four weeks and having the student meet the criteria 80 percent of the time is fine—*if* it matches and measures what the teacher expressed as the original concern. In this case, the assessment and the hypothesis don't go in the same direction.

Using the attention and focus strength chart (see Appendix A, p. 155), here is the new goal for Jerome: If we teach Jerome to use self-talk to make a plan for transitions, he will arrive at class on time. In four weeks, Jerome will go from being on time 40 percent of the time to 70 percent.

And If the Student Doesn't Meet the Goal?

If the student doesn't meet the goal criteria after four to six weeks, the teacher decides what adjustments are needed. Was the benchmark too aggressive? If the student is making good progress, does he or she just need more time? Is the goal OK, but a change in the approach for teaching and practicing is needed? Perhaps there is a prerequisite skill that should be addressed. Making any of these adjustments is fine. But a mistake we often make is making no changes at all when the student is not hitting the benchmark.

Activity 22. DATA Goal: Max's Case

Video 4.4. DATA Goal: Max's Case: https://bcove.video/3a20a08

In Video 4.4, the team is completing Max's DATA goal that Rachael started in the video in Activity 20. As you watch this clip, notice the following:

1. Were all four parts of the goal apparent and clear?
2. How did the team determine the baseline data?
3. Notice that they came up with a goal that combined both academic and executive function skills. Could they have done this another way?

Reflection questions:

1. Do your current meetings result in teachers leaving with a measurable and achievable goal?
2. How do you currently assist team members with ways to gather and record baseline and growth data?

Often academic and executive function skills are closely related. In this case, the teacher may want the two goals combined in one, as you saw in Max's case:

Hypothesis (derived from "Do" and "Achieve"): If we teach Max to ask questions and make personal connections, he will be able to recall details more easily.

Time frame: In six weeks,

Assessment: he will go from being able to make personal connections zero out of five times to three out of five (memory). He will also be able to go from recalling a key detail one out of five times to three out of five times (comprehension).

If the teacher prefers the DATA goal to be written as two separate goals, that's fine. The objective is to make the goal clear and user-friendly for the teacher. The DATA goal serves as the preview of coming attractions, a dream of what is possible. Form G is an easy-to-use tool for tracking a student's progress.

The *action plan* is the path that delivers that vision. Once the DATA goal is set, it's time to discuss the "how to" of the plan.

The Action Plan

In appreciative inquiry, the insights we glean from patterns described by the success stories about what works inform the design of the action plan. The teacher and coach select only ideas that lend themselves directly to the DATA goal. A useful strategy like "limit direct instruction time to one minute per year of student age" won't get the job done if the goal is to teach the child to write better. A strategy can be research-based and powerful, but that isn't enough. It also must match the goal.

You can practice your matching skills in Activity 23.

Activity 23. Matching Goals and Strategies: Trenton's Case

Trenton's DATA goal states:

D: If we teach Trenton to set goals and self-monitor,

A: he will reduce the number of times he disrupts the class and increase his time on task.

T: In four weeks,

A: he will reduce his class disturbances from an average of five times to two times per class. He will also increase his time on task from an average of four minutes to six minutes.

Here is the list of ideas that team members wrote down from the story Trenton's teacher told. Which are the four most powerful ideas that match Trenton's DATA goal?

The teacher will

1. Track and chart how many disruptions he causes per period.
2. Seat Trenton away from his friends.
3. Have Trenton chart his own number of disruptions and minutes on task.
4. Use a token system to reward Trenton for staying in his seat.
5. Have him complete the work he doesn't finish in the library, where Mrs. Kelly can help him.

Form G. Progress Monitoring for an Individual Student

Student Name:

What Is Being Measured	How Data Will Be Collected

Baseline Data	Week 1	Week 2	Week 3	Week 4	Week 5	Week 6	Total Growth
Academic Goal							
Executive Function Goal							

6. Have Trenton set his own goal for how long he will work on a given task without a break.

7. Send a daily report to his parents so they can reinforce the ideas of the plan.

8. Have Trenton keep a list of strategies that do and don't help.

9. Have the Title I tutor time the number of minutes Trenton stays on task.

10. Ask Trenton how he is doing on his goal and how he plans to improve tomorrow.

For the four best ideas, see the Activity 23 answer key on page 152.

Parker Designs an Action Plan for Cassie

When it was time for Parker to design his action plan, he looked at the five items that Daphne recorded on the chart paper that had worked for Cassie in the past:

1. Drawing and visuals help Cassie learn.

2. Partner work relieves stress.

3. Let Cassie try out her own thinking before jumping in and helping her.

4. Verbalizing helps her remember.

5. Having a chance to take risks privately and correct mistakes before answering makes her more confident.

He considered his projection for Cassie's future success in terms of a DATA goal:

D: If we teach Cassie ways to see and remember patterns,

A: then she will accurately complete more math problems on her own.

T: In five weeks,

A: she will go from completing zero out of five three-step problems accurately to three out of five, without assistance.

This clear goal, together with the list of what works for Cassie, made what was difficult the day before much clearer and easier. Now Parker must answer the following question: How will he teach Cassie to see and remember patterns in math? As a result of this process, he thought of several strategies right away:

1. He could tap into her drawing and sketching ability by modeling ways to use symbols and pictures to represent a math problem.

2. He could ask her to verbalize what she is learning by first drawing it and then explaining it to someone else.

3. He could suggest she use a notebook, like the one she used for soccer.

4. She could go over her visual steps before each assignment and pick the set of steps that matches the type of problem she is working on.

5. She could put examples of the type of problem that matches each drawing in her notebook to help her see the patterns even better.

Once Parker was on a roll, ideas seemed to pour out of him. Daphne suggested he look at the *What Works Clearinghouse* (https://ies.ed.gov/ncee/wwc) for additional ways to teach students to use visual representations in math. She thought the practice guide on math in grades 4–8 (What Works Clearinghouse, 2006) would be most helpful.

Daphne: You now have things you will do and things Cassie can do for herself. What ideas do you have for Cassie's parents?

Parker: I hope they will make sure she does her homework.

Daphne: Parents usually assume that teachers want them to do homework monitoring, but they often don't see that suggestion as helpful. If you can come up with something specific that helps her parents improve Cassie's memory or use of math skills at home, they will probably see that as something positive they can and will do.

Parker: How about helping with the family budget? Maybe creating a plan for how to save for a family vacation or estimating what groceries will cost once a list is made? Those are basic things, but it gives her an idea of how practical math is in everyday life. If she sees and uses her math patterns, she will be able to do those things more easily.

Daphne: Now I think you're onto something!

Parker was elated at this breakthrough and thanked Daphne as he began to pack up his things. He said that this was the most helpful 35 minutes he had spent in a long time. Daphne noted that there was one more thing they needed to do before he left—and that was to describe which step Parker and Cassie would start with immediately.

To see what the design step looks and sounds like, view the video clips in Activities 24 and 25.

Activity 24. Design Home and School Action Plans: Max's Case

Video 4.5. Design Home and School Action Plans: Max's Case: https://bcove.video/3a8IgMO

In Video 4.5, notice the following:

1. Does every idea on this plan take Max closer to the DATA goal?

2. Which ideas do you think parents will be likely to support and follow through on?

Here is Max's DATA goal: If we teach Max to ask questions and make personal connections, he will be able to recall information more easily. In six weeks, he will ask questions and make personal connections three out of five times instead of zero out of five times. He will also be able to go from recalling key details one out of five times to three out of five times. See his action plan in Figure 4.4.

FIGURE 4.4
Max's Action Plan

Things the Teacher Will Do	Suggestions for Parents	Things the Student Will Do
1. Use picture cueing cards for retell 2. Ask explicit guiding questions 3. Pause to make connections 4. Relate to previous stories	1. Use same picture cueing cards 2. Pause and check with Max while he's reading or watching TV 3. Play memory games 4. Engage in cooking activities	

Reflection questions:

1. Do you think developing a list of strategies for teachers, parents, and students is helpful? Why or why not?
2. What do you notice about the types of activities in the parent column? Are these activities typical of what you generally ask parents to do?

Activity 25. Design the Student Action Plan: Max's Case

Video 4.6. Design the Student Action Plan: Max's Case: https://bcove.video/3b5mAAC

In Video 4.6, notice the following:

1. Does each student activity enable Max to become more independent for making connections and retelling details? Why or why not?

Reflection questions:

1. How well do your action plans intentionally build in student independence?
2. What would be the advantage of expanding Max's plan to more students in the class?

Once the teacher develops a list of ideas that build on the existing strengths and capabilities of the student, it's time to decide how to launch the plan. Starting is often the hardest part. We know that trying to implement an entire plan all at once is a recipe for disaster, so "think big, start small, and begin today" is the best approach.

The commitment is both an end and a beginning in the process. It's the ending of the first coaching conversation and the beginning of the ongoing implementation and revision cycle.

Commit to an Action

We have all heard the proverb "The road to hell is paved with good intentions." The sentiment captures why each appreciative inquiry conversation closes by asking the teacher for a commitment—take one small step immediately that launches the action plan. Even for teachers with the best intentions, we know that the more time that passes without starting, the more the energy and motivation for starting are likely to diminish.

Once teachers get going, the process seems to take on a life of its own. Making a commitment to begin immediately helps people get past the hard part. That's not to imply that jumping into implementation without thinking it through is a good idea, but there's always at least a small piece of the plan that can be done right away. Things like collecting the baseline data, contacting parents to let them know your plans, or running ideas past the student are all good starting points.

> Daphne: I know you have to get to class, so we won't spend any more than six minutes on this last part. Can you tell me one small thing you will do today or tomorrow to move your plan forward?
>
> Parker: Sure. I think having Cassie draw steps for solving three-step math problems tomorrow would be a perfect beginning. Once she draws the steps, she can present the drawing to the class to get practice articulating her thinking.
>
> Daphne: I can see that strategy working eventually, but didn't you tell me that part of her problem was the stress she feels when she makes a mistake in front of her peers?
>
> Parker: Hmmm, I may be getting ahead of myself here. OK, what if she shares her drawing with a friend to try it out? Then, after she and the friend refine it, they can present it to two other students. Does that sound like a small enough step?
>
> Daphne: That sounds safer to me. You know, you could offer some options to Cassie and have her decide on what would work best. Who knows, she may come up with an option neither of us even considered. That gives you the added advantage of having Cassie own the plan with you. Making one's own choices is typically a big motivator for students her age.

The first part of the coaching process has begun for Parker and Daphne. The coach will check in with Parker occasionally to see how things are going. If it looks like Cassie and Parker have solved the problem, Daphne's responsibilities end, and she closes the case. If Cassie doesn't make enough progress, if Parker feels that he needs more support, or if another issue causes problems, Daphne will be there for Parker and Cassie. She may also need to take the process to a deeper level at that point, as described in Chapter 5.

To see how to end with a strong commitment from the team or teacher, watch the video in Activity 26.

Activity 26. Commit: Max's Case

Video 4.7. Commit: Max's Case: https://bcove.video/2ye5zWw

As you watch Video 4.7, consider the following:

1. What effect did the commitment step have on this team?
2. What coaching tips did you pick up from the way Rachael facilitated this meeting?

Reflection question:

1. How would adding a commitment step to close each of your team meetings work at your school?

Tips from the Field: In Their Own Words

Here, practitioners share their thoughts on the coaching process:

- "Our high school ends each school year by having every teacher submit a three-student watch list electronically. Our counselors, psychologists, administrators, and department heads then consolidate and prioritize this list to use as a starting place for the following year."
- "It is crucially important that the timekeeper, who is sometimes the coach in one-to-one meetings, is vigilant about informing the team or teacher about how much time is available for each step. Because timekeepers become involved in the discussion and may lose track of time, it's essential they use a timer that makes a small sound to keep the meetings focused and moving forward."
- "Using the six-step conversation guide makes this planning session flow well. When we lose sight of the flow of the meeting, we sometimes end up without a complete plan or we need a second meeting to get the work done. This is never as satisfying as leaving every meeting with an action plan."

- "We often use partner coaches to conduct these meetings, especially as new coaches are being trained by experienced coaches on the use of this protocol. Two heads are better than one when the process is new."
- "Minimizing paperwork is my favorite part of this format. This first coaching meeting has taken the place of the pound of paper we used to require teachers to fill out if they needed help with a student. We have little to no paperwork other than the notes taken at this meeting, and we have all the information we need to get started. Teachers love it!"

In a Nutshell

Teachers start each year filled with the enthusiasm and confidence it takes to make a difference in their students' lives. Every year, stress builds up as teachers face the reality that students continually present new challenges that test their skill and know-how. Who hasn't thought, "I've tried everything. Coming up with one more idea isn't going to happen this time. I've run through my entire bag of tricks, and this one has me stumped"?

The reality is, no one person has enough background experience to address every need that pops up in a classroom. The appreciative inquiry approach brings together the expertise of the parent, student, and teachers to find solutions. Teachers are always grateful when they find a realistic, practical approach to things that stress them out and a thoughtful way forward.

The coaching conversation provides a resource you can build into any existing problem-solving system. Simply put, it offers the time of a "talking partner" who knows how to create an upbeat environment and ask the right questions. The coaching conversation verifies the saying "None of us is as smart as all of us."

What if the appreciative inquiry process doesn't go far enough? Chapter 5 takes these conversations one level deeper.

Getting to the Hidden Cause with Five Whys

What if the original plan doesn't work? The purpose of the first meeting with the coach is to identify student strengths and needs and design a quick, positive action plan. That may be enough to set the student on a path for success. When problems are more complex, however, it might require a deeper dive to find hidden causes. A five whys session requires the coaching skills of listening and asking the right questions to support the teacher and student.

Three weeks after Parker began Cassie's support plan, he decided to ask Daphne to change the check-in conference from the original five weeks to three. Things were not going as well as he anticipated, and he needed to rethink the plan.

Daphne was delighted that Parker used his common sense instead of just the DATA goal time frame to decide when to resume the coaching conversation. These conversations are designed to get quick support for both teacher and student without requiring a lot of paperwork, rules, or formal procedures.

As Daphne shares the conversation guidelines for their next discussion (see Form H), Parker notices how this six-step format is basically the same as his last conversation—but with one exception. This time, a process called "five whys" replaces the focus question.

Five whys is a diagnostic conversation that uncovers what this student needs that we haven't been able to see before. The root cause then becomes the foundation for building a new DATA goal, a new success story, and a revised action plan.

Begin by Connecting

To start the conversation on a positive note and get a quick summary on the progress made, Daphne asks this connect question: "What's currently working for Cassie?" Often, unexpected benefits surface that are not being formally measured.

> Parker: Cassie is definitely happier and more willing to try different ways to solve problems. She's also articulating the math steps she needs to use pretty well. That part is happening faster than I thought it would. Cassie even agreed to explain some of her drawings to Eugene the other day. When he sincerely thanked her for her help, she lit up. Next time I ask her to do that, I don't think it will take so much coaxing. What *isn't* improving is the percentage of problems she's getting correct, and that's how I'm measuring her success on the DATA goal.

The plan that Parker developed for Cassie was strong and research based. Research (Wammes, Meade, & Fernandes, 2016) shows that visualization, especially drawing, can significantly improve memory, so Parker was totally baffled by the fact that Cassie's math grade remained a big fat *F*.

> Daphne: So it's not that the strategy didn't help in many ways. It did. Several important executive function skills are getting stronger. Congratulations on that! Now we need to take the next step and find out what less obvious academic or executive function skill is missing and standing in the way of Cassie's improvement in math. Are you ready to expand the action plan?
>
> Parker: Absolutely. I was so sure the first plan would work. This is frustrating.

Use the Five Whys

When great solutions don't work, it usually means there's an aspect of the student's problem we're not seeing clearly. Parker is ready to explore what adjustments will help Cassie move forward. Is the pace too fast or too slow? Is the environment too demanding or too protective? Is the lack of certain prerequisite skills creating a gap that prevents Cassie from moving forward? Is there some other mysterious cause? It's time for Daphne to drill down using five whys to open up new possibilities.

Five whys is a Six Sigma tool developed by Toyota for problem solving. By asking *at least* five iterations of "why," this technique systematically peels away surface symptoms to reveal underlying root causes. Each answer the teacher gives is the basis for the coach's next why question. This questioning sequence continues until a new way of looking at the problem comes to

Form H. Five Whys Coaching Conversation Guide

Date:	Coach:	Teacher:	Student:
Purpose	To dig deeper into the root cause in order to design new learning opportunities		
2 min.	**Connect:** Tell me what progress has been made since the last time we talked?	Strengths you see in this student and progress made since last coaching meeting:	
20 min.	**Review focus concerns and use five whys** to find the hidden skill needed.	Academic concern (in teacher's words): Executive function concern (in teacher's words):	Hidden skill identified by five whys (see strength charts): Hidden skill identified by five whys (see strength charts):
4 min.	**Establish a DATA goal:** If you apply what you know to this situation, what could happen in six or fewer weeks?	**D**o: If we teach _____ to _____, **A**chieve: we will see this outcome _____. **T**ime: In ___ weeks, **A**ssessment of growth: _____ will go from _____ to _____.	

5 min.	**Share success stories:** Ask the teacher(s) to describe a time when a student was successful learning this skill.
	  1. What did the student do?
	  2. What did the teacher(s) do that helped?
	  3. What did the parents do?
	  4. What did the other students do?
		Ideas from your success story:	How does this strategy affect student thinking?

5 min.	**Design an action plan:** Based on this story, what ideas fit this student best?	Things I will do: Suggestions for parents:	Things the student will do:
4 min.	**Commit to an action:** What small step will the teacher act on tomorrow to move the plan forward? What will happen the following week? How will this skill be monitored?	How I will start tomorrow:	How I will monitor progress:

light. To see an example of how the five whys works in everyday life, watch *Five Whys Jefferson Memorial Example* (ASQTV, 2016) at www.youtube.com/watch?v=BEQvq99PZwo.

The best results happen when you use five whys to analyze both the executive function and the academic symptoms together. It doesn't matter which you start with. Coaches often begin with executive function because those issues tend to be more exasperating and emotional for teachers. Students may not have an academic problem, but 100 percent of them benefit from executive function support. Moreover, every academic problem is connected to some type of executive function delay.

In Cassie's case, Parker is already seeing success in several executive function areas. Her memory for steps and procedures is improving, and she's happier and more verbal when she works with a friend. Her willingness to try new strategies and risk sharing with other students is a little stronger, but it's still an area that needs improvement. Because Cassie's motivation to keep working is now strong, Daphne decides to start the five whys by focusing on math skills.

It's important for the coach to start by explaining the what and why of the five whys process before beginning the conversation. Knowing there will always be at least five questions—no matter how good the teacher's answer is—lowers the teacher's level of anxiety.

> Daphne: Before we begin the five whys, I will explain the reason for doing it. We need to discover a new piece to Cassie's learning puzzle. That means we have to keep digging until we identify a factor that has not been obvious up to now. Naturally, this part of the conversation feels more challenging than our previous ones, but just hang in there with me. It will be worth it. One thing you need to understand is that even when you give perfect answers, the why questions will continue at least five times. That should get us to the new root cause. If we need to go more than five whys, we will. That sometimes happens in tough cases.

Stating these facts up front helps teachers know what to expect and keeps the process from feeling like an interrogation. The communication skills of the coach have a huge effect on how well the five whys process works.

Six Tips for Successful Five Whys Conversations

Daphne keeps these important tips in mind as she conducts this conversation.

1. Build All Questions on What the Teacher Just Said

The first question the coach asks should address the student symptom. For example, if the teacher says the problem is student note taking, the coach would ask, "Why is he having such a hard time taking notes?" The coach listens carefully to the teacher's response and builds on the teacher's answer. If the teacher responds, "Paul just can't keep up," the coach's next question is, "Why do you think he can't keep up?" That's the pattern throughout the entire five whys questioning process. Keep it simple by using as few words as you can when asking questions.

2. Make the Questioning a Conversation

Even though every question needs to be an analysis-type question, when questions all start with the word "why," the conversation begins to sound stiff and stilted. This often results in feelings of defensiveness that shuts down insightful thinking. Daphne always asks why something is or isn't happening, but she looks for a variety of ways to phrase this so the discussion remains conversational.

For example, instead of asking, "Why is Maria struggling with organization?" she asks, "What secret do other students know about organization that would help Maria find her papers quickly?" or "What could be causing this organization problem?" These questions always help the teacher stay inside the student's head for the answer. Although every question is getting at a why, they shouldn't all start with the word "why."

Here are some helpful sentence starters:

- Why do you think . . . is happening?
- What could be causing . . . ?
- What is interfering with . . . ?
- What could other students teach the student that would help this problem?
- What skills might this student be lacking?
- And you think the student does that because . . . ?
- What makes . . . so hard for the student?
- What might be another reason for . . . ?

3. Listen with the Intent to Understand

Daphne needs to make sure she understands the teacher's response, so she uses paraphrasing to reflect what she thinks she heard. Paraphrasing isn't just restating a teacher's words; it's restating what you think the teacher means, but in your own words. For example, if the teacher says, "Paul can't take notes because he can never find his materials," Daphne might be confused about what the teacher is implying. Her paraphrase might sound like this: "You think, then, that Paul has the skill to take notes. He just has nothing to take notes with." This enables the teacher to clarify which type of problem Paul has: organizing material or organizing thoughts. Paraphrasing moves the analysis forward and keeps communication clear. Daphne trusts that teachers will correct her if her inference is incorrect.

As the why question/answer sequence repeats, Daphne listens carefully for clues and patterns that uncover root causes. Because she knows what information is on the strength charts, she listens carefully for statements that point to a need for any skills listed there. She is also alert to things that take the conversation in unhelpful directions, like moving out of the circle of influence, making value judgments, and jumping to solutions.

4. Stay in Your Circle of Influence

Let's say the teacher blames the family for not providing support with homework. If Daphne asks, "Why isn't the family supportive?" this conversation is officially going out of the teacher's circle of influence. Teachers are not in charge of family dynamics; continuing that discussion ends up making the teacher feel hopeless and helpless. Even when statements that are critical of the family, the student, or the teachers from last year hold an element of truth, blaming simply identifies a culprit and doesn't uncover root causes that we can do something about. Not helpful.

Here are some of the most common statements coaches hear that lead to unproductive conversations:

- The family doesn't value education.
- Nobody is there to help at night with homework.
- She's a special ed student.
- He has a memory disorder.
- She has a low IQ.
- He's been in four different schools in three years.
- She doesn't get enough sleep. She stays up all night playing video games.
- There's abuse happening in that family.

Not talking about these issues during the five whys conversation doesn't mean they're unimportant. It means we need to help the child build coping skills, and we need to turn the rest of the problems over to people—the nurse, the psychologist, the administrator, or family services—who have the power and position to help and support in different ways.

5. Move Past Value Judgments to Specific Observations

Making value judgments about a student's character is just as unproductive as going out of your circle of influence. Value judgments typically are both subjective and vague, and therefore they need clarification. For instance, if Daphne asks, "Why do you think Janet chooses to horse around rather than do her work?" the teacher might respond with a value judgment of "She's just lazy or unmotivated." This points out the teacher's opinion of this student's character flaw instead of focusing on the student's thinking or the skill deficit that perpetuates this behavior. Again, not helpful.

Before asking the next why question, Daphne clarifies the value judgment by asking, "What do you see Janet doing that makes you think she's lazy?" The teacher may respond, "She refuses to hand in her work on time." That's a specific symptom we can use to drill down to possible causes. By refocusing on specific behaviors or skills that can be taught, the conversation is more likely to uncover helpful root causes.

6. Avoid Premature Problem Solving

As hard as it is to prevent value judgments from derailing the diagnostic conversation, generating solutions prematurely is the toughest stumbling block of all. All day, every day, educators must come up with hundreds of quick solutions. When you ask teachers to switch their thinking to diagnosing, the habit of jumping to solutions often interferes. Daphne tries not to exacerbate this problem by asking questions like "What have you tried?" or "What would happen if you did ___?" These questions are great during the story or design conversations, but they cause real problems during the five whys segment. Daphne assures teachers that taking the time to identify the root cause first will result in more powerful solutions later on.

Activity 27. Five Whys: Cassie's Case

Let's take a look at a five whys conversation. As you read it, notice the following:

1. Daphne uses what Parker is saying to develop her next question. She uses Parker's words and then asks a question that helps Parker play the role of Cassie's mind reader. She doesn't ask what Cassie is doing or what kids sitting around her are doing. She asks about what is going on in Cassie's head that makes her do or think the way she does.
2. Daphne listens for new strengths while reminding Parker of things he learned from their last conversation that can help develop the action plan later on.
3. Daphne tries not to be wordy as she asks her questions.
4. Daphne will record her questions and Parker's answers on Form I or Form J so she can retrace her steps if she decides to redo any parts of the conversation.

Daphne: You're concerned because Cassie's math accuracy on three-step problems isn't any better than it was three weeks ago. Why do you think that hasn't improved?

Form I. Five Whys Conversation: Academic Concern

Build your questions on the teacher's answer and use paraphrasing. Question starters: • So why does he . . .? • What is interfering with . . .? • What else could be causing . . .? • What is it that makes ___ so hard for him? • This happens because . . .? • What do other students say or do in their head that helps them with this? End with: • So are you saying . . .?	**Academic concern:**_____		
	Coach says	**Teacher says**	**Clarification**
	1.	1.	
	2.	2.	
	3.	3.	
	4.	4.	
	5.	5.	
	6.	6.	

Form J. Five Whys Conversation: Executive Function Concern

Build your questions on the teacher's answer and use paraphrasing.	Executive function concern: _____		
	Coach says	**Teacher says**	**Clarification**
Question starters: • Why does she . . .? • What do other students think about that he doesn't? • What is it that makes ___ so hard? • This happens because . . .? • What do other students say or do in their heads that helps them with this? • What else could be causing that? End with: • So are you saying . . .?	1. 2. 3. 4. 5. 6.	1. 2. 3. 4. 5. 6.	

Parker: I don't know. The memory strategy helped her keep the steps in her head, so I thought that would make the difference. It didn't. Her answers are still wrong.

Daphne: What causes her answers to be wrong?

Parker: She makes lots of basic computation errors.

Daphne: And that's happening because . . .

Parker: Hmmm. She knows her facts fairly well, so I guess they're just careless errors.

Daphne: You said before that Cassie still cares about learning, so what would be the reason for the careless errors? What's going on in her head, in your opinion?

Parker: I really don't know. Maybe "careless" wasn't the right word. I don't see her as not caring, but I can't think of another reason for these consistent mistakes. That's what's so frustrating.

Daphne: Let's take a look at this strength chart on math [see Appendix A, p. 159] and see if you can verify her strengths and perhaps pinpoint one or two areas that might be causing the problem.

Parker: This *is* helpful. I'm seeing several areas where Cassie is doing well, and some I'm not sure of. We already know about her reluctance to ask for help, and that's improving. I do think her computation mistakes are related to place value. That may be the key I've been overlooking. She really should have learned that in 2nd grade.

Daphne: I can't tell you how many times I've thought just that: Wouldn't it be nice if every student learned on schedule? We know that's not how it works though. That's why we need tools like five whys to figure out where those gaps are. What's keeping her from learning place value now?

Parker: I suppose there are two reasons. I haven't really taken the time to reteach it this year, and she probably needs to apply her new visualizing strategies so she gets it this time.

Daphne: Great. Because you've identified place value as the hidden stumbling point, I think you have a new DATA goal for your action plan.

Parker: I think so, too. It's going to be this: "If I teach Cassie to understand place value through visualization strategies, she will improve her accuracy in computation." You know, I just thought of another reason Cassie might be making those "careless" mistakes. I think she's freaking out whenever she's tested. She does much better in class, but she blows it on quizzes.

Daphne: Perfect. It helps when you can put yourself in Cassie's place and try to see what might be happening in her head. So the DATA goal now becomes "If we teach Cassie ways to become fluent with place value through visualization and to calm herself during quizzes, she will correctly compute more math problems." How long should we give her this time, and what measurement will you use for growth?

Parker: I think I'll go four weeks this time, and how about using the same growth measurement as before? "She will go from completing one out of five three-step problems accurately to three out of five without assistance."

Daphne: Sure, and for the academic part you might want to add that Cassie goes from making _____ place value errors to _____ . Are you also measuring how well she's able to calm herself before and during quizzes? That way you can give her feedback on both skills.

Parker: Yikes, how do you measure that?

Daphne: Probably the best way is to ask her to rate herself before a quiz on a Likert scale from 1 to 5. You could even use emojis to make it quick and easy. Then ask her how she calmed herself.

Parker: Easy enough. All right, so the last part of the DATA goal now says, "In four weeks, Cassie will do three things: Go from averaging one out of five to three out of five three-step problems correct, go from making whatever her baseline is on place value errors to _____ , and improve her stress level from an average of _____ to _____ on a scale of 1 to 5 before and during quizzes." It would be good to have her jot down what strategies work for her when she's anxious, too. I can reach out to the counselor, get some ideas for self-calming strategies, and pass these on to Cassie. That's a lot of things to address, but each data collection is quick and easy, so I think she and I can handle that.

Daphne: Let's sketch out simple report forms for Cassie to use for herself. That way she can measure her own progress and then decide if she needs to make changes to her plan. We want her to take ownership and credit for her own growth.

Reflection questions:

1. What was one thing that Daphne said that helped clarify the questioning process for you?
2. How did the initial conversation in Chapter 4 help this conversation get a more complete picture of Cassie's needs?
3. How did Daphne help Parker turn his conclusions into a clear DATA goal?

Figures 5.1 and 5.2 show the self-monitoring forms that Parker and Daphne came up with in Activity 27.

FIGURE 5.1

Self-Assessment Rubric for Measuring Level of Stress

How Stressed Am I?	1	2	3	4	5
Before the quiz					
During the quiz					
How I calmed myself					

FIGURE 5.2

Cassie's Weekly Progress Monitoring Chart

Student Name

What Is Being Measured				How Data Will Be Collected			
Steps correct, place value errors and ability to self-calm before and during quizzes				Daily work for math and a self-assessment on a Likert scale for stress level changes before and during quizzes			
Baseline Data	Week 1	Week 2	Week 3	Week 4	Week 5	Week 6	Total Growth
Academic Steps correct on 3-step problems	1 out of 5 steps correct						
Academic Number of place value errors	Average of X place value errors per paper						
Executive Function Improvement score for self-calming	Rating X to X now						

Let's pause now to view the five whys conversation in Activity 28.

Activity 28. Five Whys: Max's Case

Video 5.1. Five Whys: Max's Case: https://bcove.video/2xl2pAg

As you watch Video 5.1, observe how the coach facilitates each part of the five whys conversation. Consider the following:

1. How is the connect question different from those you have seen before?
2. How did Rachael get Amanda to narrow the focus for this conversation?
3. What points did the coach make when explaining the process of five whys?
4. How did Rachael move away from the answer that went out of the circle of influence?
5. Name three different ways Rachael started her five whys questions to make the questioning more conversational.

Reflection questions:

1. What are the similarities and differences between this five whys conversation and your team's problem-solving conversations?
2. How did using the strength charts help?

Now it's time for *you* to try your hand at analyzing five whys conversations. The practice exercises in Activities 29 and 30 will increase your awareness of what to look for in a productive five whys conversation.

Activity 29. Spotting Key Points in a Five Whys Conversation

Read the coaching conversation that follows to identify the following coaching strategies:

1. Four ways the coach asks the why question without saying "why."
2. One paraphrase he uses for clarification.
3. How the coach handles the teacher's judgmental statement.
4. How the coach keeps the conversation from jumping from executive function issues (reasons why Terry gives up) to academic issues (Terry's writing problem).

Coach: Why do you think Terry gives up so easily?

Teacher: He's just not motivated.

Coach: Because there's always a reason for low motivation, what do you think makes him want to give up in your class?

Teacher: Sometimes he just sits and stares, and then he starts goofing around with people sitting close to him.

Coach: And he decides to goof around instead of starting his work because . . .

Teacher: Because he's avoiding doing his assignments.

Coach: Why do you think he wants to avoid assignments when there are negative consequences to that?

Teacher: I don't think he believes he can do well, so he just doesn't try. But really, he's very capable.

Coach: So you're saying that if he can't get an *A*, he doesn't want to try? Are we talking about a perfectionist here?

Teacher: No, "perfectionist" doesn't fit, but I do think lack of self-confidence is part of the problem. Actually, he struggles with getting his thoughts on paper. He's fine orally, but writing things down is the real problem.

Coach: I'll note that we should address the writing problem when we get to the academic five whys, but now let's go deeper into Terry's lack of belief in his own ability. What do you attribute that to?

Teacher: I don't know what causes lack of self-confidence. Maybe it's his home situation.

Coach: We can start with the strength chart on problem solving [see Appendix A, p. 164] to help identify both Terry's strengths and growth opportunities that affect self-confidence. See if any of these ideas fit:

- Is he overwhelmed and doesn't know how to break things down into bite-size pieces?
- Does he set realistic goals for himself?
- Does he think that his effort, skills, and strategies simply result in more failure and that it's not worth the risk of being embarrassed?
- Does he see grades and feedback on mistakes more like a punishment than feedback? He might not give himself credit for small successes.

Teacher: Any of those could be the answer for Terry. I want to choose all of them.

Coach: We want to make sure you don't overextend yourself or Terry. If we write the first part of the DATA goal so it includes several of those points, the goal statement would read, "If we teach Terry to break tasks into manageable chunks, set goals for himself, and track his own progress, he will see that his efforts pay off in growth and he will complete more work." Can the two of you handle all of that at once? Limiting how many things we work on simultaneously is a wise decision. Of course, we can apply the DATA goal and action plan designed for one student to an entire group with similar needs. That would make the extra effort easier to handle.

Reflection questions:

1. At what point in the conversation did you see the teacher switch from blaming the student to understanding that there is a skill that needs to be taught?
2. What useful coaching pointers did you take from this conversation?
3. Use the strength charts to identify a specific skill needed by one of your own "unmotivated" students.

Strength Charts and the DATA Goal

If the teacher cannot come up with an answer to a why question, the strength charts offer many possibilities. In the video in Activity 28 (p. 95), you saw how Rachael referred to the strength charts to move the conversation forward and transition from five whys to the DATA goal. These charts are helpful in two ways: They identify skills the student already has and pinpoint areas that need to be strengthened. By uncovering missing or weak skills, the teacher often spots new learning opportunities that could unleash student potential.

These charts are beneficial as long as they are not introduced into the conversation too soon. The coach always explores the teacher's insights about the student *before* offering a tool that could possibly sidetrack important thinking. Save the charts for after you have asked at least three why questions. Introducing them too soon may take the teacher down the wrong path. Let the teacher keep what he or she thinks is going on in the student's head as the primary way of drilling down to the root cause. It's not necessary to use the charts at all if the teacher is able to identify unexplored causes without them.

In Activity 30, we will look at how the teacher and the coach create a new DATA goal for Max.

Activity 30. New DATA Goal: Max's Case

Video 5.2. New DATA Goal: Max's Case: https://bcove.video/2Rxlvc3

As you watch Video 5.2, consider the following questions:

1. How is Max's DATA goal connected to the five whys?
2. What question does the coach use to help Amanda determine the second part of the DATA goal (both the time frame and assessment measure)?
3. How is the fact that Amanda doesn't have hard baseline data on Max for these two skills (follow-through on two-step tasks and be able to retell details about text features) going to affect the DATA goal?

Reflection questions:

1. What would you see as the best and easiest way to collect data on your students' growth in following two-step directions and retelling text features?

2. How could you involve your students in the data collection and reflection?

3. How could using this DATA goal format help your team write clearer, more measurable goals?

Troubleshooting Coaching Errors

Because the success of this process totally depends on the coach's listening and questioning skills, we will now present you with a more challenging task. Activity 31 offers two scenarios in which the coach makes errors in the questioning process. Find ways to fix the problems. Good luck—and may the Force be with you.

Activity 31. The Five Whys Session: Where Did the Coach Go Wrong?

In the two scenarios below, the coach's mistakes in questioning take the five whys session off course. Identify specific errors the coach makes. How would you rectify them? Compare your answers with the answer keys on page 153.

Scenario 1: Haley is in the middle of 1st grade and still doesn't know her letter sounds:

Coach: Why do you think Haley is having such a hard time with her letters?

Teacher: She doesn't pay attention in class.

Coach: Why doesn't she pay attention?

Teacher: People around her are making too much noise.

Coach: Why are other kids making so much noise?

Teacher: They're doing different work than Haley is.

Coach: Why is Haley sitting at the table with kids who are doing different work?

Teacher: She gets to choose where she wants to work.

Coach: Do you think she would do better if we assigned her a quiet spot to work?

Scenario 2: Jose acts like the class clown during science class. He makes wise-cracks, falls out of his chair, makes fun of other students, and sometimes sings loudly while working.

> Coach: What's causing Jose to act so silly during science class?
>
> Teacher: He craves attention because he lives with his grandparents and they aren't strict enough.
>
> Coach: Do you think his rivalry with his brother is the main cause?
>
> Teacher: No. He knows he's cute and bright, and he wants to manipulate everyone.
>
> Coach: So why doesn't he know about boundaries?
>
> Teacher: When most 8th graders act this way, a subtle cue is enough to make them stop. He just ignores my cues.
>
> Coach: Why doesn't he pay attention to your cues?
>
> Teacher: He wants attention, or maybe we aren't making the consequences stiff enough.
>
> Coach: Why aren't your consequences stiff enough?

Sometimes a coach has a hard time figuring out why the conversation is skipping all over the place. One of the most common reasons is because the teacher didn't really answer the coach's question and the coach didn't realize it.

The Executive Function Five Whys

Like most teachers, Parker is comfortable analyzing missing academic skills. Experience and a skills progression chart help teachers identify academic gaps. The discussion always gets trickier when the next question is something like "*Why* do those skills continue to be missing?" Generally, it's not that the skills haven't been taught well. It frequently comes down to which executive function needs keep the academic skills from sticking or which instructional strategies work better for this student than the ones used initially.

When coaches start with academics, they need to follow up by doing the five whys process on the executive function needs as soon as possible. This takes the whole child into account. The executive function five whys can happen during the same session, or you can reschedule that conversation for another session if time is short. Teachers are often surprised to see how much easier it is to solve problems after looking at the student's situation from both angles.

Parker's second planning conversation goes fairly quickly because in the previous meeting, he decided that using visuals and having Cassie articulate her learning addressed her memory needs for remembering steps and patterns. That same plan works well for teaching place value. By adding a few new resources, the academic plan is solid.

Now that they have completed the five whys and have set the DATA goal, Daphne supports Parker in developing strategies that help him begin right away.

Eliciting Stories That Work—And Why

Daphne listens to and records Parker's favorite techniques for teaching place value, as well as ideas he has heard from other teachers (see Figure 5.3). She adds a strategy she found on What Works Clearinghouse. It's called CRA (Witzel, 2009), which means the teacher works from concrete to representational to abstract. This technique is especially good for teaching place value and fractions, and it fits perfectly with Cassie's strength of responding to visuals. One item on the list that follows also addresses Cassie's need to self-calm.

Committing to a Plan

Daphne will now conclude the meeting with a clear commitment plan from Parker and check to see if he needs a commitment from her or anyone else to go forward. After Parker connects the idea of anxiety and the missing place value skill with what he already knows about what Cassie responds well to, he develops and commits to another great action plan.

Daphne: What part of your plan will you start tomorrow?

Parker: I'm going to take a look at how to implement that CRA idea with place value. I'll do that tomorrow, and I'll start using it with Cassie on Monday. I also plan to talk with the counselor about ideas for how students can self-calm before quizzes.

Daphne: Good. By the way, what communication have you had with Cassie's parents lately?

Parker: Because we moved up this coaching conversation, they're not expecting to hear from me for two more weeks.

Daphne: I ask because teachers often request a student support meeting when initial plans don't produce the results they're hoping for. These meetings get the family face to face with staff to develop an expanded and unified plan for both classrooms and home. People who have tried it are amazed at how positive and helpful it is. [See Chapter 6 for details on the student support meeting.]

Parker: Let me try the CRA strategy and see how that goes. In two weeks, I'll probably be ready to include the parents and Cassie in a joint meeting.

Daphne: Let's meet next week so I can walk you through the steps for prepping the parent and student for the meeting. You've been a resource person for other teachers' student support meetings, so I know you'll be comfortable with the meeting itself.

FIGURE 5.3

Story Notes for Cassie: Place Value and Self-Calming

What Works for Place Value and Self-Calming?	Why It Works
1. Expanded notation activity: Give Cassie a number like 2,321, and she lays it out on her desk using base ten blocks or graph paper squares. Then she fills in the place value chart. 	Thousands	Hundreds	Tens	Ones
---	---	---	---
1000	100	10	1
1000	100	10	
	100				It visually and representationally shows what Cassie knows about place value.
2. Use the same chart to show addition and subtraction with composing and decomposing numbers.	This activity broadens the visualization of the original chart to help her articulate how to break numbers down and regroup them in a variety of patterns.
3. Play a card game where student partners draw a number like 2,486. Both partners draw from a pile of thousands, five hundreds, hundreds, fifties, tens, fives, and ones cards until they can lay out the exact number. (We'll add decimals later.)	This activity adds the element of fun to practicing expanded notation as well as to composing larger numbers from smaller ones.
4. Concrete representational abstract (CRA) from What Works Clearinghouse.	It helps with visualization of hard concepts.
5. For self-calming, Cassie can have a fidget tool on her desk or something she thinks will help.	It allows her to choose a way to self-calm and gives her ownership.

Doing the five whys adds a lot to a teacher's insights into new learning opportunities, but it's not the typical way most educators have been taught to look at learning and behavior. The more you practice, the easier it gets. Drilling down always challenges our perspective and opens up new possibilities for learning.

Common Questions Asked—and Answered

Here are some questions that practitioners typically ask as they familiarize themselves with the five whys process.

How Much Time Should the Five Whys Conversation Take?

Asking the five whys generally takes about 20 minutes to cover both academic and executive function issues. The first five whys session usually takes longer than the second five whys session because many of the answers that have surfaced in the first meeting apply to both areas. When teachers are comfortable with the process and the coaches are well versed in the strength charts, this process goes much faster and is easier.

What If the Teacher Doesn't Answer the Why Question?

Let's say the coach asks, "Why isn't Carmen getting her work done?" and the teacher responds, "She just sits there and daydreams." The teacher has offered interesting information, but she didn't answer the question. If teachers describe what the student is *doing* instead of what the student is *thinking*, the five whys won't work well. So what should a coach do?

First of all, coaches need to be aware that the answer didn't match the question. To keep the drill-down conversation from going sideways, ask the same question with slightly different phrasing—for example, "Why do you think Carmen daydreams instead of doing the assignments?" Occasionally, telling teachers to pretend to be a mind reader helps them focus on what's going on inside the student's head rather than simply describing symptoms. Attempting to see inside the student's head for answers is the secret to successfully finding the root cause.

How Will I Know When to Stop?

The drill-down questions of the five whys continue until the teacher and coach agree that they've uncovered a root cause that the teacher wasn't seeing before. We want the teacher to leave seeing this student through a new lens. Sometimes this takes 15 whys, but once everyone gets used to the process, 5 or 6 why questions typically do the trick.

What If the Teacher Can't Think of an Answer?

At times, teachers get stuck and can't think of an answer to the why question. In that case, the coach should pause to see whether the teacher just needs a bit more time to think. If think time isn't the issue, the coach is free to suggest two or three skills from the strength charts as possibilities. Make sure you have asked at least three why questions before you start making suggestions to the teacher. Trying to "help" the teacher too soon stops their reflective process.

If the teacher says, "I don't know" *before* the third why question, think of a way to rephrase the question or give a different prompt, such as "If you could make a wild guess, what would you say?" or "Can you think of a specific skill that might be missing?" If the teacher says, "I don't know" *after* the third why question, the coach is sometimes also at a loss. In that case, use the strength charts in Appendix A (pp. 154–170) to help. The more familiar you are with these charts, the easier the five whys conversations become.

Tips from the Field: In Their Own Words

Here's what practitioners have to say about the five whys process:

- "Remember to ask questions that help the teacher read the student's mind. Ask questions like 'What's causing this student to react that way?' or 'What do other students know to do that this student has yet to learn?'"
- "Having two coaches is an even bigger benefit for doing the five whys than it is for other types of conversations. We like to put a content person, like a reading teacher, with a process person, like a counselor or special ed teacher. This combination makes the questioning much easier."
- "The more familiar a coach is with the strength charts, the easier it is to hold a five whys conversation. Regular practice helps you see patterns that are helpful."
- "Every couple of months I ask a teacher if I can videotape our coaching session so I can reflect on the kinds of questions I'm asking. I can think of options during the reflection that don't occur to me when I'm asking questions in a real conversation. This helps me hone my coaching skills."
- "We used to get bogged down by requiring teachers to collect a pound of data before entering the process. Now a coach helps us pinpoint the exact type of data that would help us monitor the progress of the student."
- "If at the end of the five whys conversation, the teacher says, 'That's exactly what I thought the root cause was,' then I know I didn't do the five whys correctly. I probably stopped too soon. The root cause is always something the teacher didn't suspect."
- "Our schools have one coach per grade level or department, and that's perfect, but we don't limit these people to working only with their group. Sometimes it's better if the coach doesn't know the student, especially in cases where discipline is an issue."
- "I find that holding coaching conversations with individual teachers is the easiest format, but multiple teachers can add a depth of knowledge about a student that a single teacher cannot see. The problem with multiple teachers at a five whys meeting is the tendency to take the conversation in multiple directions, resulting in a hot mess. To solve this, I ask one teacher to be the spokesperson and the others to give a thumbs-up if they agree, a thumbs-sideways if they partially agree, and a thumbs-down if they don't see the student the same way. This generally solves the problem."

In a Nutshell

In Chapters 3 and 4, we saw how to use the appreciative inquiry approach to facilitate individual teacher, student, and parent conversations. Many times, these are the only conversations needed to get an effective intervention plan in place. For more complex cases, the coach may decide to add the five whys process to the conversation before starting the success story, action plan, and commitment.

The purpose of this process is to see the problem through the student's eyes. This may be difficult and frustrating at first because it's not the typical approach to problem solving. This deep dive into the student's situation pays off by uncovering root causes of issues in both academic and executive function areas that must be addressed for the intervention plan to be successful.

It can be difficult for coaches to be sure they've reached the correct root cause. Before you assume you're finished asking a teacher why, *ask yourself* this:

- Is the identified root cause something the teacher already knew was the problem? If so, you're not finished. Ask a few more why questions until you come to an aha moment—a new way of thinking about this problem.

Also, *ask the teacher* the following questions:

- "If this root cause is addressed, do you believe it will significantly improve the student's progress?" If the teacher gives a half-hearted answer, you probably need to go back and keep drilling down.
- "How is this different from what you tried before?" If you decide to implement a strategy that the teacher has already used, it's unlikely to work. It's imperative that you approach the instruction and practice in a new way, one that fits the student's profile better than the original technique.

This is just like practicing medicine. Doctors are only sure the diagnosis is correct when they see that the treatment works. Sometimes the original diagnosis focuses on the wrong thing, or sometimes the diagnosis is correct but identifies just one part of a more complex issue. It may take a few tries to get it right. You never can be sure that you have the right root cause until you see the positive results of the intervention.

Chapter 6 looks at ways to hold a totally positive and powerful intervention planning meeting that involves the parent, student, and selected faculty members.

The Student Support Team Meeting

Parker's novel ways of teaching place value unlocked new doors for Cassie. Her math accuracy and her ability to remember math steps both improved. She wasn't averaging three out of five answers correct, but growth was happening. The new aspect of stress management turned out to play a bigger part in Cassie's memory and error problems than anyone had suspected.

As Parker discussed Cassie's progress with the other 6th grade teachers, Julia mentioned that Cassie also struggled to remember information in science. Sharonda chimed in to add that she saw the same thing in social studies. Parker had piqued the interest of the other teachers in becoming involved in the coaching conversations. All three teachers decided to talk to Daphne about the possibility of holding a student support team meeting to come up with a unified plan for Cassie.

Activity 32. Student Support Team Overview

See if you can answer the following questions after reading the dialogue and the discussion below:

1. Who is invited to student support team meetings, and why is the number limited?

2. How long are these meetings, and what enables them to be short and productive?

3. What ground rules and routines guide these meetings?

4. What process is used to select the action plan during a student support meeting?

Parker: Hi, Daphne. I brought Sharonda and Julia with me to talk about holding a student support team meeting. I've been sharing what I've learned about Cassie's strengths and learning preferences, and they have used a few of the strategies. Now they have some questions for you.

Julia: Yes, the idea of drawing and explaining steps to another student did help in science, and Cassie likes it. But we move pretty fast in that class, and I'm afraid she's missing too much because of the time it takes her to draw.

Sharonda: Same in social studies. We have tons of content, and I wonder if this drawing thing will get old after a while.

Daphne: I love that you are all focused on providing Cassie with a learning opportunity that plays to her strengths, but you're right, Sharonda. We don't want to get stuck on just one way of doing things. What you need is a wider variety of memory strategies— and a student support team generates just that. It provides lots of options in a short amount of time that apply to both home and school. It lets us surround the student with consistent support.

Julia: So what does this meeting look like, and who should be there?

Daphne: Anyone who makes sense. We need enough people to create a solid plan without having the size of the group feel intimidating to Cassie and her parents. Usually five or six people is the max. Cassie, her parents, and the three of you would be plenty.

Sharonda: What about you? Don't we need a coach with us? Typically, we include a special ed teacher and the psychologist.

Daphne: If you want me to guide you through the first meeting, I can do that, but the format is simple and positive. I think you can do it yourselves fairly easily, especially because Parker has been involved before.

As for involving special ed teachers or the psychologist, it's not called for at this point. The teachers haven't implemented enough Tier 1 classroom interventions to indicate the need to jump to more intense levels. They can always change the makeup of the team if different needs emerge. The bottom line is this: Invite as few people as possible, but make sure they're the right people. For example, if the goal targets reading strategies, invite a reading expert. If the student has a medical issue, invite the nurse or drug therapist. Instructional needs can be addressed by adding current or former teachers who have been successful with the student in the past. And teachers can certainly consult with other faculty members beforehand and bring valuable advice or strategies to the meeting. This brings a wider variety of ideas to the table without requiring the physical presence of those experts.

Sharonda: So what happens during this meeting?

Daphne: Basically, it's about a 25-minute session of brainstorming followed by the selection of strategies for action. There is absolutely no conversation about problems or side issues. One hundred percent of the time is focused on specific strategies that bring the student closer to the DATA goal.

Julia: How do you get people to cooperate with the rule about "all talk is about solutions and not problems"? It's so ingrained to do the opposite.

Daphne: It's tricky at first, but I've found that going over the guidelines before we start each meeting is helpful. Also, the structured meeting agenda keeps the session flowing quickly and in a positive direction. People understand that not talking about the problem is what keeps the environment safe and welcoming for the student and the parent and sometimes even the teacher. That particular guideline is essential.

Sharonda: So are there any other guidelines for this type of meeting?

Daphne: Yes, other than "absolutely no talking about the problem," we begin and end on time, we follow the structure of the agenda, and each of us comes prepared with at least three interventions.

An agenda might look like this:

- Review the DATA goal to set the purpose for the meeting: 2 minutes
- Brainstorm ideas in three categories (home, school, student): 12 minutes
- Select the action ideas for home, school, and student: 5 minutes
- Review how the data will be tracked and recorded: 4 minutes
- Set the date for the follow-up meeting: 2 minutes

Everyone in the meeting comes with three suggestions that match the DATA goal—one idea for school, one for home, and one for the student. For example, Cassie would bring an idea for how she would like to see her parents help her, which she would place in the parent column, as well as an idea for how her teachers could help, which she would place in the school column. Then she adds one idea in the student column for how she can help herself. The teachers and parents do the same, adding one idea for each of the three categories. All ideas are recorded on chart paper (see Figure 6.1) so the list of possibilities to choose from is visible to everyone. If everyone has come prepared to this meeting, each person will have six or seven ideas in their column, some of which may be generated on the spot.

FIGURE 6.1

Recording Sheet for Possible Strategies

DATA Goal:		
Ideas for School	**Ideas for Home**	**Ideas for the Student**

The key aspect of any productive meeting is maintaining a positive and supportive relationship among the members. When the coaching conversation develops a clear DATA goal in advance, everyone understands the purpose of the meeting so there is no reason for it to go off the rails by focusing on problems instead of solutions.

Here are the meeting "rules of the road":

- We begin and end all meetings on time and follow the timed agenda.
- The meeting focuses only on collecting and organizing ideas that support the student in reaching the DATA goal. If necessary, additional discussions can be held after the meeting adjourns.
- During brainstorming, clarifying questions are helpful; judgments about the value of ideas are avoided.
- Each person chooses one or two ideas from his or her own column to commit to. If you do not like an idea recorded in your category, you are under no obligation to choose it as part of your action plan.
- All members bring their calendars so a follow-up meeting can be scheduled before the meeting ends.

- If people violate these guidelines, we agree to respectfully call them on it.

Sharonda: What was that about choosing ideas from your own column?

Daphne: The teachers choose from the school column, the parents select from the home column, and the student selects from the student column. No one is permitted to choose for someone else. That was one of the mistakes we used to make in our old system. Teachers would ask the parents to do a certain activity, like help with homework, and then be disappointed if the parents didn't follow through. Sometimes parents didn't follow through because they couldn't. They often agreed in the meeting because they didn't want to appear uncooperative. The same thing happened to teachers at times. When people choose their own way to be part of the plan, they choose what is realistic for them.

Sharonda: What if they say there's nothing on the list they can do?

Daphne: That's highly unlikely because they put at least one of the ideas in their column.

Julia: What if the parent suggests an idea for my school column that isn't realistic, like "do private tutoring every day" with their child?

Daphne: You graciously write their idea on the chart to show that you hear and respect their thinking. No need to say, "Are you serious? I have 28 other kids in the room!" You simply do not choose that idea as your part of the action plan. Remember, you control your own column—but only your column. Everyone commits to helping the student move forward in the way they think is best. This respect for one another pays off in many ways.

Julia: What if the parents don't come with any suggestions, or what if they don't show up at all?

Daphne: We don't miss a beat. We just proceed with whatever ideas we have with whoever does show up. There's no time to waste when it comes to supporting students and teachers.

Reflection question:

1. How do the guidelines and routines in this meeting compare with those you currently use in your school?

Parent Involvement

One thing that keeps the process positive and productive is the school's intentional effort to make the parents and students an integral part of the system. So many times, frustrated teachers say something like, "We're killing ourselves trying to help these students, and the families aren't taking their part of the responsibilities seriously. This is nuts!" We conducted an interview with teachers to find out why they think parents don't attend problem-solving meetings. Here are their top three responses:

- "They don't value their child's education."
- "They can't or won't take the time to come to school."
- "They're frustrated and don't want to face the problem."

When we asked parents why they are sometimes reluctant players, here are some of their answers:

- "I'd rather have a root canal than go to another meeting with teachers. I've heard the list of my kid's problems for six years running with no results. I can't take another meeting like that."
- "I hated school when I was there. I'll be darned if I'm going there now."
- "I want to go, but I don't have transportation."
- "Some teachers don't seem to care about anything but grades and rules. I have no desire to have that discussion again."
- "I don't have anyone to watch my preschoolers."
- "Some teachers treat me like I don't get it. The fact is, they really don't know my child and how hard things are for her right now. They think I'm just making excuses for her."
- "Tell them what's bothering me? What if I do, and they take it out on my kid?"
- "I cannot attend during the workday. I have to save those days off for times when my kids are sick. The teachers don't understand that parents who are hourly wage earners are docked for taking time off."

These are the kinds of comments parents make at scout meetings and ball games. The polite version that educators hear sounds more like "Sorry, but I can't make that meeting" or "Did I forget that meeting?" Whether you hear the straight story or the other version, the message is the same: Our parent involvement practices need to be more user-friendly.

It's easy to criticize parents and students for not stepping up to the plate, but often we fail to build the type of support system that makes active family involvement more likely. At every meeting, parents need proof that our intention is to help their child, not just report problems. Research (Henderson & Mapp, 2002) supports the idea that parental participation improves both students' academic and behavior achievement. We need this solid partnership.

Partnerships take work but are absolutely worth the effort. When we go beyond thinking of parent involvement as organizing fundraisers, volunteering, helping with homework, and enforcing school rules, things get better. These activities are valuable, but they tend to cast parents as backup rather than involving them in the decisions that directly affect their child's learning opportunities.

When parents feel that what they say is valued and used, an attitude of trust and cooperation flourishes. This does not happen overnight. It takes frequent and consistent action over several years to convey the message to the community that parents and other caregivers are welcome and honored here.

Here are a few suggestions that increase parental attendance at meetings:

- Parents are more likely to attend meetings they see as valuable for their child's learning. Be specific about what you intend to accomplish and how you and the parent can make learning happen by working together.
- Feeling welcome requires that the parent clearly understands what you're saying. Slow down, don't use educational jargon and acronyms, and provide a translator for parents who are not fluent in English.
- Focus the meeting on building new skills based on the student's existing strengths and interests, not on fixing what's wrong with the student.
- Reassure families that they're not the only ones who have struggled with this type of issue. Together you can help their child cope with difficulties and learn new strategies.
- Provide transportation to parents without transportation, or consider making a home visit.
- Offer childcare for younger siblings so the parent can relax and pay attention during the meeting.
- Acknowledge the value of the things the parent has done so far to help their child.
- As unreasonable as their requests may appear, remember it's the parent's job to protect and defend their child and see that he or she gets what they need. Don't say anything that smacks of "You have to understand that I have 28 other students in the room, so I cannot possibly do ___ for your child." Let them know that helping their child is your primary goal.
- Many parents cannot leave work without placing the family finances or their continued employment on the line. Consider phone or FaceTime alternatives for parents who cannot come to school.
- Tell parents the meeting will last for 20 to 25 minutes, and keep your promise.

Prepping for the Meeting

Cassie's three teachers prepared for the student support meeting by finding strategies for their classrooms, for home, and for Cassie. All the ideas built on Cassie's strengths and addressed the needs outlined in her DATA goal.

To identify the specific place value skills Cassie missed in earlier grades, Parker started by looking at the following YouTube video (Battelle for Kids, 2014) on the importance of using vertical progression guides: www.youtube.com/watch?v=AKbhYqmadNA. He also located two wonderful video resources: the Teaching Channel (www.teachingchannel.com) for classroom ideas and Khan Academy (www.khanacademy.org) for student activities.

Parker knew Cassie would love this lesson from Khan Academy (n.d.) on understanding place value: www.khanacademy.org/math/pre-algebra/pre-algebra-arith-prop/pre-algebra-place-value/v/understanding-place-value-1-exercise. She could do these lessons at home in place of her regular homework, and they could go over the concepts quickly the next day. He thought that several other students would respond well to this approach and that they could become a study group. Parker also talked to Mrs. Williams, the math consultant, to see what ideas she had to offer.

> Mrs. Williams: I'm going to define *basic math skills* as more than just being fast and accurate with traditional facts. Choosing the correct strategies and applying them in numerous ways are just as basic as memorizing facts. How well does Cassie come up with equivalent sums by composing and decomposing using mental math? For example, how many ways can she solve $7 + 9$? Can she come up with ideas like $1 + 9 + 6 = 16$, and $6 + 4 + 6 = 16$? Those would be the two easiest ones because they look for tens combinations as the first step. Looking for doubles and then adding or subtracting more is another key strategy. So $7 + 9$ could be thought of as $7 + 7 + 2 = 16$ or $9 + 9 - 2 = 16$. These are the basic skills that good math students do in their heads regularly to become fluent at solving math problems.
>
> Parker: I have no idea if Cassie uses these skills, but my guess is she doesn't.
>
> Mrs. Williams: I can screen Cassie for these basics and make suggestions.
>
> Parker: Can you do this screening on several students? Also, I'd like to observe you so I can add this new way of diagnosing to my own skill set.

Parker also read a research article (Klemm, 2016) the counselor gave him that said that oversecretion of stress hormones impairs recall. One book by Fisher and Frey (2014) stated that stressed students perform worse and forget more of what they have learned. That certainly sounded like it fit Cassie's case.

Teaching Cassie to become more aware of her own body signals for signs of stress would help her know when she needs to use self-calming techniques. Parker decided to have her make a list of typical signals of oncoming stress, like shallow breathing, muscles tightening, fast heart-beat, squinting, clenching fists, and so on. Once she had the list, she could use it to check and rank her stress level.

Parker asked the counselor about strategies for relaxation and positive self-talk. He liked her idea of having Cassie write down all her negative thoughts before and during quizzes and then overwriting them with positive messages (see Figure 6.2). Once she learns to catch herself doing self-talk that increases her anxiety, she can create new habits of positive self-talk to decrease it.

The ideas Parker found applied to the home, school, and student, so it would be easy to coordinate efforts. If the other two teachers found as many specific ideas as he did, this meeting would go well.

FIGURE 6.2
New Habits for Self-Talk

When Do I Usually Do This?	Negative Self-Talk	Positive Self-Talk
As I am studying for a quiz	I probably won't do this right tomorrow.	What parts am I good at?
As I am taking the quiz	What if I make a mistake?	I choose to grow from fixing my mistakes.
When I come to a hard problem	I never get this part right.	I will try new strategies until I figure this out.
After the quiz	I'll never be good at math.	I am definitely getting better at math. I can do this!

Preparing the Parent for the Meeting

Parker was glad he had established a positive working relationship with the Ramirez family in previous conversations. That made calling to prepare them for the next meeting much easier. He was confident he wouldn't forget what he needed to say because Daphne provided him with specific parent talking points.

Parent Preparation Talking Points

- State the purpose of the meeting by explaining the DATA goal. Make sure to send a written copy as a follow-up.

- Go over the format of the meeting and the Rules of the Road. Remind the parent that they have a copy of the rules on the back page of their school handbook. Send home an extra copy of the rules with the DATA goal attached.
- Make sure the parent knows exactly who is invited to the meeting and why those people were asked to attend.
- Agree on a date, time, and place for the meeting.
- Explain the parent's assignment of bringing three suggestions for supporting Cassie to the meeting: one for themselves, one for teachers, and one for Cassie. Tell them that you will send a list of things other parents have suggested in the past to get them started but that they should feel free to come up with their own ideas.
- Tell them that someone will make a courtesy call in the next day or so to answer any questions they may have or help them if they want more suggestions or ideas.

Activity 33. Preparing the Parent: Cassie's Case

As you read this dialogue between Parker and Mr. Ramirez, see if all the key parent preparation talking points are covered. Is there anything you would add or change about this conversation to make it more effective?

Parker: Good afternoon, Mr. Ramirez. This is Parker West, Cassie's math teacher, calling.

Mr. Ramirez: Hi, Parker. Is something wrong?

Parker: Actually, Cassie is making a lot of progress during math class, but we still can't get those grades up. I decided to talk to one of our problem-solving coaches today, and I think we've uncovered something new. I noticed that Cassie does much better in class than she does on quizzes, so we're thinking that her stress level on testing days is causing a big part of her problem.

Mr. Ramirez: That certainly sounds right. Cassie hates to make mistakes, and she gets so wound tight when she has a test that she almost makes herself sick.

Parker: I'd like to invite you and your wife to meet with our team to plan a new level of support for Cassie.

Mr. Ramirez: You're thinking she's special ed?

Parker: No, I really should have said *classroom support*. In our student support meetings, a group of teachers meet with the parents and their child to design ways of learning new skills that apply to both home and school. Don't get me wrong—we can use this format for students in special ed programs, too, but testing and special ed placement aren't what this meeting is about. In Cassie's case, her plan will continue focusing on using her strong visual skills to strengthen her memory, but we're going to expand the plan. Because stress is a factor that messes with memory, we want to develop a plan to teach her ways to relieve her own stress as well.

Mr. Ramirez: I'm for anything that would help her. It's hard to see her so frustrated.

Parker: Because the science and social studies teachers are seeing similar stress in Cassie in their rooms, I'd like to invite them to be part of our group. Our team would be just the three of you and three of us.

Mr. Ramirez: Sure, that sounds right. I wonder why the English teacher isn't having the same problem.

Parker: I was wondering the same thing. I'll check with her and see if I can steal a few of her ideas for helping Cassie and bring those to our meeting.

Mr. Ramirez: You say Cassie will be at this meeting? That ought to make her stress-o-meter spin off the charts. Do you really think that's a good idea?

Parker: Our ground rules for this meeting make it safe for all kids and adults to attend without fear of embarrassment or being put on the spot. One rule is that none of us will talk about problems at all. We spend 100 percent of our time identifying ways we can support Cassie, and she spends her time telling us ways she would like to be supported. Nothing else is on the agenda.

Mr. Ramirez: School has certainly changed since I was a student. If you were called to a meeting with your parents, you knew it was going to get ugly.

Parker: Ugly is the opposite of what we're after here. At this 25-minute meeting, each person brings three ideas for helping Cassie: one idea for teachers, one for parents, and one for Cassie to do for herself. Because there are six of us, we'll have 18 ideas in about 12 minutes.

Mr. Ramirez: You're going to give me 18 ideas to do at home?

Parker: No, only six or so will be in your home column. You and your wife can choose one or two ideas from your column that you're willing and able to do. I know you already help her a lot. This just gives you more possibilities. One of the ideas in your column will be your own suggestion, so I know there will be at least one that you like.

Mr. Ramirez: I'm supposed to bring an idea, too?

Parker: Yes, family and faculty members are equal partners on this team. We each have an opportunity to suggest things that we think will help Cassie. We write every idea on a separate sticky note and put them on chart paper in either the home, school, or student column, then we each choose an idea to implement from our own column.

Mr. Ramirez: I think I'm out of my league here. I could help you with your taxes, but I can't tell you how to teach math or manage stress.

Parker: Your suggestions don't have to be specific teaching ideas. You're the expert on your daughter and on how to make learning easier for her. Think back to your favorite teacher or things your mom did for you that relieved your stress and motivated you to learn. Those are the kinds of ideas we need to hear from you. I can send home a list of ideas other parents suggested as their children worked on these same problems.

Mr. Ramirez: Definitely, send the list.

Parker: I'll send the ideas, a copy of Cassie's goal, and a sheet with our Rules of the Road on it. You already have our meeting rules on the back page of your school handbook, but I generally send another copy in case you can't lay your hands on the handbook.

Mr. Ramirez: What are those meeting guidelines?

Parker: The main points are that no one will talk about problems and that we'll all share ideas for helping Cassie. By the way, if I slip up and bring up a problem like a missing assignment, feel free to stop me. If you bring up a problem, I'll do the same for you. We want Cassie to leave knowing that we're all on her side. Our meetings are about support and about taking action to solve problems, not just talking about them.

Mr. Ramirez: We could use that motto at my office.

After arranging a date, time, and place to meet, Parker mentions that someone will make a follow-up call to see if the parent has any questions or needs any help. This follow-up call emphasizes the importance of parent involvement and catches miscommunication and potential problems and misunderstandings before they get a chance to derail the meeting.

Activity 34. Preparing the Parent for the Student Support Team Meeting

Video 6.1. Preparing the Parent for the Student Support Team Meeting: https://bcove.video/2RA5YJp

The parent preparation can be done by phone or in a face-to-face meeting. As you watch Video 6.1 of a parent preparation meeting, refer to the parent preparation talking points (pp. 113–114) to see whether all the key points are covered.

Reflection questions:

1. How does this resemble the way you currently prepare parents for meetings?
2. Following this call from the school, what do you think the parent's conversation might sound like?
3. Would you approach anything differently? Explain.
4. What is one tip you could give this teacher to make the parent conversation even better?

Preparing the Student for the Meeting

Successful student involvement in the support meeting depends on how well the student is prepared. Typically, the classroom teacher walks the student through the process, explaining what to expect and demonstrating the student role. In cases where the student and teacher have a rocky relationship, a coach or another teacher can assist with this premeeting session.

Addressing the student talking points that follow is key to a successful meeting.

Student Preparation Talking Points

1. Clarify the DATA goal, who will attend, how long everyone will meet, and the meeting Rules of the Road.
2. Make certain the student knows that he or she has both voice and choice and that adults and students will honor each other's ideas.
3. Explain that everyone has the same assignment: to bring three ideas for accomplishing the DATA goal.
4. Help students come up with an idea for teachers, an idea for parents, and an idea for themselves. Write each idea on a separate sticky note or, in the case of a young child, draw a picture of the idea.
5. Select a tool for the student to collect and display the data. Clarify what is being measured and how that information is used.

Activity 35. Preparing the Student: Cassie's Case

As you read the following dialogue between Parker and Cassie, watch for these points:

1. How did Parker make Cassie comfortable enough to have an authentic discussion?
2. What points about the student support meetings did he make sure she understood?
3. What is the major difference between the student and the parent preparation for the meeting?

Parker: Hi, Cassie. How do you feel about the progress you've made in the last three weeks in math?

Cassie: OK, I guess. [Pause.] I still have a *D*.

Parker: That's true, but I think you know more than the math quizzes are showing us. I have a feeling that your nerves are getting the best of you, and that's why you have a hard time remembering what to do on quiz days. Actually, that happens to many people.

Cassie: Really? Nerves can do that?

Parker: Sure can. So here's what we can do to help. We have meetings called student support meetings where parents, teachers, and kids get together and design a plan that helps. It's a lot like what you and I did together before, but more people will help this time.

Cassie [worried voice]: My parents have to come to school? But I'm trying really hard.

Parker: Don't worry, it's not a "call you out" kind of meeting. No one will say things that embarrass you. We're all happy with your progress, but we want to help in new ways. At the meeting, everyone comes with three ideas for helping you in math or with your nervousness about tests. There will be no talk about problems, just solutions.

Cassie: What if they can't find a way to help? I think I'm just a nervous person, and no one can change that. I don't think I'll ever be good at math, either.

Parker: We won't give up until we figure it out. It's your job and my job to keep trying until something does work. You know, negative thinking and worrying can be turned around. Lots of people do it, and once they succeed, they amaze themselves with what they accomplish. It'll be hard work, but it's worth it. Are you in?

Cassie: I'll try. What do I have to do?

Parker shows Cassie several ideas for stress management and for learning place value and for composing and decomposing numbers.

Cassie: I can use the rating scale for stress while I'm studying, and I like turning negative self-talk into positive. Can I choose both?

Parker: Sure. Now what suggestions do you have for your parents and for me?

Cassie: You're kidding, right? I'm supposed to tell *you* what to do? Wait, I think I might need help figuring out the positive words. Can you and my parents help with that?

Parker: Absolutely. See, you have your three ideas, plus an extra one for yourself. Let's write those thoughts on separate sticky notes so you have them ready for Monday's meeting. When it's time for you to explain your ideas, just stick these on the chart under home, school, or student. We'll all do the same thing with our ideas, and once all the notes are up, you may choose the idea you like best from your own column. Your parents and I may or may not choose the idea you put in our columns. We each get to choose what we think will work best.

Cassie: Can I choose more than one thing?

Parker: Sure, but try not to start too many things at once. That never turns out well. If you choose something and it doesn't work, you're free to change your mind. You're in charge of improving, so do what you think will get the best result. I have some tools you can use for tracking your own growth [see Figures 6.3 and 6.4]. See which ones you think will work best.

Reflection questions:

1. How do you include students in planning their own interventions?
2. What ideas from this scenario could be used to strengthen your process?

Figures 6.3 and 6.4 are two monitoring tools—a stress rubric and a self-monitoring tool—that Parker showed Cassie for tracking her stress levels.

FIGURE 6.3

Self-Assessment Rubric for Measuring Level of Stress

How Stressed Am I?	1	2	3	4	5
Before the quiz	😄	🙂	😐	🙁	😧
During the quiz	😄	🙂	😐	🙁	😧

To see an example of a student being prepared for a student support team meeting, watch the video in Activity 36.

Activity 36. Preparing the Student: Maddie's Case

Video 6.2. Preparing the Student: Maddie's Case: https://bcove.video/2V6L4Ea

Refer to the list of student preparation talking points (p. 117) to see if the teacher in Video 6.2 covered each point, then consider the following:

1. Notice how the teacher accepts and extends the student ideas.
2. What did the teacher do to help this student buy into the process?

Reflection questions:

1. How do you think the student felt at the conclusion of this meeting? Why?
2. What is your plan if your student can't come up with any ideas?

FIGURE 6.4

Self-Monitoring Stressors

Period	What stressed me?	How I chose to handle it	On a scale of 1–5, how well did it work?
First period			
Second period			
Third period			
Fourth period			
Homework time			

Students need to understand that they are in control of their own learning and that adults want to support them. When students participate in the design process, they tend to cooperate more and appreciate what's being done. This is a big change from many of the old models where the student felt victimized by the process or was completely left out.

The entire team is more likely to come prepared and follow through if the goal is clarified by specifying exactly what evidence each person should collect to determine the success of the action plan. The teacher, parent, and student need a way to measure growth in small increments. This is known as *progress monitoring*.

Progress Monitoring Guidelines

The purpose of progress monitoring is to

- Show the current level of academic or behavior performance (baseline data) and then systematically measure the student's progress toward the DATA goal.
- Determine the effectiveness of instruction or of the intervention plan.
- Guide instructional decisions and adjustments.

Let's look at Rebecca's case to understand the thinking behind how progress monitoring works.

Rebecca: A Focus on Reading Comprehension

Seven-year-old Rebecca has difficulty with reading comprehension. After completing the appreciative inquiry interview with the coach, her teacher, Miss Wood, remembered that when she prompted students to answer *who, what, when, where, why,* and *how* questions while reading, comprehension usually increased. She is going to intensify the use of this strategy by using visuals and connecting concepts as described in this website from James Madison University: http://coe.jmu.edu/learningtoolbox/5w1h.html.

So Rebecca's DATA goal is this: "If we teach Rebecca to answer *who, what, when, where, why,* and *how* questions using visuals, her comprehension will increase. In five weeks, she will go from correctly answering _____percent of comprehension questions to _____percent."

Miss Wood isn't sure where Rebecca's starting point is, so she collects baseline data by looking at work samples from the previous five weeks. Baseline scores must always be stated in measurable terms (for example, current words per minute, scores on a rubric, percentage correct, number of minutes of sustained behavior, or level or number of prompts needed to sustain a behavior). This baseline then serves as a starting point for measuring growth. Research suggests collecting a minimum of three to five data entries to establish a credible baseline (Wehby, n.d.) .

Here's how Miss Wood calculated Rebecca's baseline score for *who, what, when, where, why,* and *how* questions. Based on the last five main idea and detail worksheets, the percentage of comprehension questions that Rebecca answers correctly now ranges between 20 and 40 percent. Averaging the five scores determines her baseline of 31 percent. Once the DATA goal has a baseline score, Miss Wood sets a target goal. Rebecca's DATA goal now reads as follows: "If we teach Rebecca to answer *who, what, when, where, why,* and *how* questions using visuals, her comprehension will increase. In five weeks, she will go from correctly answering 31 percent of comprehension questions on main idea and details to 50 percent."

Research shows that the most successful students are those who are actively involved in their own learning (Center for Teaching and Learning, n.d.). By creating a bar graph (see Figure 6.5), Miss Wood enables Rebecca to track her own progress. When Rebecca explains which strategies work for her and which do not, she sees how her effort and the new strategies pay off. This reflective conversation helps develop a growth mindset (Dweck, 2016). Rebecca will learn to celebrate her successes and help her teacher make decisions about when and how to adjust her instruction.

Which Type of Graph Is Best?

A line graph is the most common visual used for tracking academic or behavior growth. The individual data points connected by a line create a visual display that makes it easy for students to evaluate whether they are or are not improving on a particular skill or behavior.

Miss Wood chose a bar graph to help Rebecca track her own progress because bar graphs are easier for young students to create and read. The bar graph enables Rebecca to be actively engaged with her data by coloring in the bars after Miss Wood marks the point that shows her score. At the end of each week, Miss Wood asks Rebecca the following reflective questions based on her data chart:

- What are you practicing, and why is it important?
- Do you think that what you are doing is helping you get better? Explain what's working.
- Is there anything you and I need to do differently next week?

FIGURE 6.5

Bar Graph for Progress Monitoring

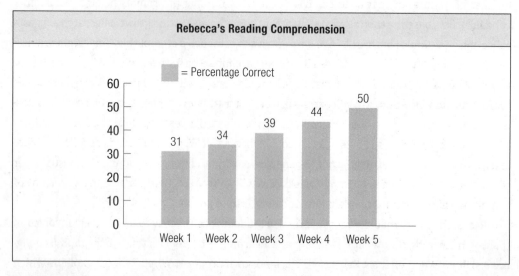

Teaching students to self-monitor by guiding them through a reflective process based on data is a crucial life skill.

What Should We Measure?

It's best to think of measuring in three basic ways:

- **Frequency** measures the increase or decrease in the number of occurrences.
- **Duration** measures how long a behavior lasts.
- **Intensity/quality** measures how much better or worse something is.

Figure 6.6 shows how this might look with a student who has regular meltdowns.

Notice how Sally is not expected to instantly change. The plan is for reasonable growth in small steps over time. When she achieves these goals, new ones will be set to help her extinguish the unproductive behavior and replace it with new and more helpful ways to respond to her stress. Measuring and displaying small, consistent steps of growth are keys to long-term success.

If Olympic swimmers measured their athletic performance in minutes shaved off their time, they would seldom see their own progress. Instead of minutes, they measure in increments of seconds or hundredths of seconds. This is the kind of thinking needed for effective progress monitoring.

FIGURE 6.6

Frequency, Duration, and Intensity: Tracking Sally's Meltdowns

Concern	Frequency	Duration	Intensity
Temper tantrums	Change in how many tantrums in a day	Change in how long each incident lasts	Change in how loud and disturbing this is
	Sally will go from having 10 tantrums a day to 5.	Sally will reduce the amount of time being upset from 20 minutes to 10 minutes per episode. *Or* Sally will be able to calm herself enough to be able to resume her work within 45 minutes (currently it takes her about 75 minutes).	Sally will go from screaming and kicking to removing herself to a cool-down place and writing or verbalizing how she feels.

For example, the number of words written per minute is better than pages completed, the number of steps completed in a math problem is better than just looking at a final answer, and the number of steps in a process that the student can explain correctly is better than assessing whether the entire process is right or wrong. This concept of measuring in small units is important if we want students to maintain enough motivation to keep trying.

Here is a checklist to guide progress monitoring design:

- Are you measuring frequency, duration, intensity/quality?
- Is the assessment short and easy to administer?
- Is the assessment repeatable so you don't compare apples to oranges?
- Can the student see growth at a granular level (very small increments)?
- Is the data easy to record and visual enough to easily draw conclusions?
  ◊ Bar or line graph
  ◊ Chart
  ◊ Rubric
- Does the assessment measure the change you want to see?
- How often will you monitor progress?

Data Collection Tools: An Overview

Now that you know what to look for, let's go through some of the tools that make data collection quick and straightforward.

Rubrics

Rubrics measure quality or intensity. A well-designed rubric clearly communicates academic or behavior expectations. Rubrics also provide a detailed list of the sequence of skill progressions that are helpful for setting small goals for growth. Figure 6.7 shows a rubric for measuring collaboration.

The video *Accessing and Using Rubrics Inside SLP Toolkit* (SLP Toolkit, 2018) gives an added explanation for the rationale of creating rubrics: available at www.slptoolkit.com/blog/rubrics-video. It also provides additional progress-monitoring rubrics for both academic and behavior issues.

Videos

With videos, you can measure frequency by using tally marks, duration by using a timer, and intensity or quality by pairing it up with a rubric. John Hattie (2012) lists *microteaching* as having a huge effect (0.88 effect size) on student growth. In microteaching, a teacher

FIGURE 6.7

Rubric for Collaboration

Traits	1	2	3	4	Points
Participates	Rarely focuses on the task and what needs to be done.	Focuses on the task and provides ideas and solutions some of the time. Is a willing participant on the team.	Focuses on the task and provides ideas and solutions most of the time. Is a strong participant on the team.	Focuses on the task and provides ideas and solutions for projects. Encourages and supports other members' ideas.	
Is Dependable	Is late most of the time, is unprepared, and misses all deadlines for turning in work.	Is late some of the time, is sometimes prepared, and frequently turns in work after the deadline.	Is on time, turns in most work on time, and asks for help when unable to fulfill team responsibilities.	Is prepared, turns in all work on time, and is very self-directed.	
Is Encouraging	Has difficulty listening and is unwilling to consider others' ideas. Is often negative.	Has some difficulty listening and tends to dominate discussions. Is sometimes positive.	Actively listens and asks questions when he or she does not understand. Maintains a positive attitude.	Respectfully listens, asks questions of all members. Helps the group reach consensus. Maintains a positive attitude.	
Is a Productive Team Member	Depends on other team members to do his or her assigned role.	Performs a few duties of the assigned role.	Performs most of the duties of the assigned role.	Knows the role and understands how fulfilling it affects the success of the team.	

videotapes part of a lesson with the intention of improving a specific teaching skill or technique. Later, the teacher views the taped lesson with a trusted colleague to analyze what went well and what to improve. This same thinking can be applied to assessing and giving feedback to students.

For example, take Henry, a 4th grader who interrupts the class frequently. He's oblivious to the fact that his outbursts of shouting and moving around the room happen frequently. By videotaping a segment of a class period, the teacher gives Henry the opportunity to see himself in action. By using a rubric (see Figure 6.8) or tallying the frequency of certain behaviors, Henry becomes more aware of his current level of activity, as well as its effect on others. By tallying his number of outbursts and then comparing clips over time, he can determine how much growth he's making. He then can make appropriate adjustments to his improvement strategies.

Checklists

Checklists generally are used to measure steps completed as you check off items; they can also measure quality if accompanied by a rating scale. For example, a checklist for satisfaction with a hotel experience may have five items to look for, as well as a rating scale on how pleased you were with the quality.

In an article titled "Check It Out! Using Checklists to Support Student Learning," Kathleen Dudden Rowlands (2007) suggests how to use checklists to assess student progress. She explains that a well-designed checklist takes a complex task and breaks it down by listing individual parts. This makes diagnosing strengths easy for the teacher. It also enables the teacher to pinpoint the exact area where a process breaks down.

Task-based checklists have the added bonus of helping students follow steps, feel in control, stay focused, and become accountable for the learning. Intervention Central (n.d.) offers a Self-Check Behavior Checklist Maker that teachers can use to design behavior checklists tailored to specific students' needs. You can access this tool at www.interventioncentral.org/tools/self-check-behavior-checklist-maker.

Work Samples

Of all the progress monitoring tools, work samples are one of the easiest to use. Work samples can measure frequency (how many complex sentences you recognize), duration (how long you worked on a task), or quality (how many strong points you made and backed up with evidence as you wrote the paper or delivered the verbal argument). The best part of using work samples is that these are everyday activities. There is no interruption of instruction and no time spent creating a new tool.

FIGURE 6.8
Sample Line Graph for Frequency: Tracking Henry's Outbursts

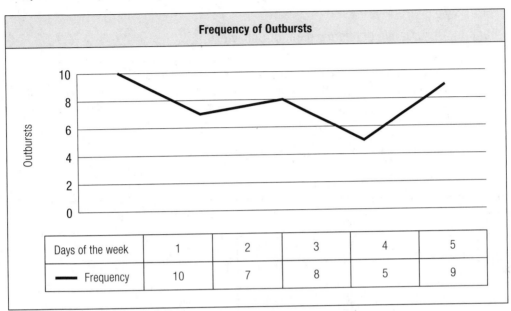

You really don't need anything fancy. You can use daily work to see patterns of progress. A math paper that contains the same level and type of problems as other math papers is perfect as a weekly growth check. The same holds true with written work. Pick out three paragraphs from a written paper and check for complete sentences and correct grammar each week. This is often better than using a test of grammar because it checks for application in context.

The easiest mistake to make when using work samples is failing to check for consistent and comparable skills. For example, you cannot track comprehension accuracy if the questions on one work sample address recall and the next assignment has inference questions. You must check for the same level of difficulty and the exact same skill set. Two-step math problems are not the same as three-step problems, and dividing whole numbers isn't the same skill as dividing fractions.

Observations

Observations can measure frequency, duration, and intensity/quality. They also make a perfect pairing for all of the tools noted. Once a checklist or rubric defines what quality looks like, it's easy to use observation to check for those skills in a skit, video, conversation, or performance. Observations bring strengths, needs, and next steps to the forefront more authentically than written work does, especially if the student has weak writing skills. Figure 6.9 shows a rubric that easily lends itself to observation. Observation using an app like Zoom is critical to distance learning so that you know who is answering the question or doing the work.

FIGURE 6.9

Rubric for Observation of Improvement of Behavior

	Screams and kicks publicly	Quiets down but refuses to move	Moves willingly to the calming corner	Is willing to verbalize or write about feelings
Mon				
Tues				
Wed				
Thurs				
Fri				

All the great monitoring tools and display graphs in the world are worth nothing if you don't use the data to make decisions about what to do next. So how do you know if the strategy you have chosen is effective or if you need to revise it? You use the four-point rule.

The Four-Point Rule: See What Is and Isn't Working

When using this rule, the teacher looks at the four most recent data points. If all four points are above the goal line, you can raise the goal. If all four points are below the goal line, you need to change the intervention or instruction (Searle, 2010).

Figure 6.10 displays a progress chart showing the four-point rule with respect to digits correct in the answer to the math problem. The diagonal line represents the goal line. You will notice that the early weeks of instruction are working. Between week five and week eight, however, a continual drop occurs, indicating a need to change instructional strategies. The vertical bold line drawn at week eight signifies that a change is made, and the new strategy is noted at the top of the graph (self-monitoring to identify errors). The data go on to show that the new intervention is working because the data points consistently trend at or above the goal line.

FIGURE 6.10

Progress Chart Showing the Four-Point Rule

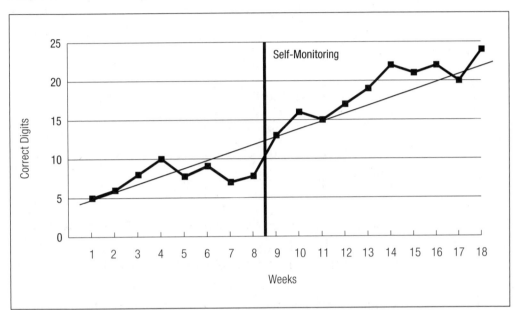

One or two drops below a goal line could mean a bad day or bad prompt, but four consecutive points below the line is a clear signal that a change of strategy is needed. After week 13, this teacher could consider raising the goal line because the rule of four states that four consecutive data points above the goal line may indicate a need for more challenge.

You have tools for collecting data, graphic display options, and a rule to help you interpret the results. Now it's time for the practical application of all this work: the student support meeting.

The Student Support Meeting

If all of the premeeting work is skillfully carried out, all team members are fully aware of the purpose for meeting and have selected strategies that support the student goal. Everyone is primed for success. Whoever decides to be the coordinator handles introductions, makes welcoming remarks, assigns roles, and reviews ground rules and the DATA goal to focus the group. Then all members explain their ideas and place their sticky notes in the proper columns (home, school, student). This takes about 10–12 minutes. As each person chooses a strategy for implementation, the selected sticky notes are moved to the bottom of the chart.

To see an actual student support team meeting in action, view the video in Activity 37.

Activity 37. Student Support Team Meeting: Maddie's Case

Video 6.3. Student Support Team Meeting: Maddie's Case: https://bcove.video/2xlHRaR

As you view Video 6.3, consider the following:

1. List three things you noticed that contributed to a safe and welcoming environment.
2. How did the use of sticky notes aid in the flow of the meeting?
3. How did the coordinator keep the team focused on the student's DATA goal?
4. What do you think the parent would say if asked to give feedback on how this meeting was handled?

Reflection questions:

1. Could your problem-solving meetings use any of the ideas you saw in this video?
2. Look at the completed student support team meeting summary (see Form K). Is this enough of a summary to help everyone remember what their commitment is between this meeting and the next? Would you add any information?

Strategies and progress monitoring ideas and tools are clearly identified in the meeting so the parent, the teacher, and the student can track the student's progress from various perspectives. These data are then shared at the follow-up meeting and become the basis for deciding what happens next.

Follow-Up Meeting

After the meeting, Parker reviewed Cassie's choices of strategies and monitoring tools. She decided on two tools to get herself started—one for home use and one to use in all of her classes. Cassie chose to monitor her stress levels in all classes by using Figure 6.3 every time she had a quiz or test. She will talk to Parker about what self-calming strategies work best for her. She decided to go to yoga classes on Thursday nights with her mom to learn new breathing and self-calming techniques.

Parker scheduled five-minute check-ins twice a week with Cassie to discuss how well the plan was working. During this check-in they compared their data, celebrated successes, and decided if anything in their plan needed to be tweaked. At first, Cassie was unhappy about having to chart her data and check-ins. It took time away from other things she needed to do. Parker explained check-in sessions to Cassie this way:

Form K. Student Support Team Meeting Summary

Student:

Date:

Concerns	**Hidden Skill(s) Needed**
Not completing multistep problems correctly	Be able to visualize patterns and steps and explain or draw the steps

DATA Goal:

D: If we teach _Maddie__ (student name) to ___ visualize steps before starting to solve the problems ___ (new skill),

A: He/she will be able to ___ complete more multistep problems accurately ___ (change in student behavior or learning).

T: Within ___ four weeks ___ (time frame; not more than six weeks),

A: He/she will go from ___ doing 3 out of 12 problems accurately ___ (baseline score) to 6 out of 12 ___ (predicted amount of growth).

School Strategy	**Home Strategy**	**Student Strategy**
1. Perform check-ins on agenda with a homeroom teacher regularly. 2. Teach her to use a checklist to double check her visualization of steps.	1. Apply the three-step visualization skill to home tasks.	1. Utilize her agenda. 2. Review new content steps for 10–15 minutes a day.
School Monitoring	**Home Monitoring**	**Self-Monitoring**
Number of correct responses on multistep problems for classwork	Number of correct responses on home tasks	Charting the number of correct responses for home and school tasks twice a week

Next date to meet: November 6, 2020

Parker: Let's think of these data check-ins as taste tests. Say you wanted to be a contestant on the show *Cupcake Wars*. Wouldn't you keep tasting your cupcakes to see if your new recipes are good enough? Without taste tests, you'd be throwing new ingredients together and just hoping people liked the new product. That's risky business because some combinations could be nasty. By tasting, you would probably be able to guess what changes it would take to make your cupcakes award winning. That's what we're trying to do here as we talk each week.

Cassie: I'd rather eat cupcakes, but that does make sense. If I'm going to be an award-winning stress manager, I need to check my ingredients and results regularly, right?

Parker: You're a quick study. And after *four* weeks, the two of us will meet with the entire team again to share our results. Then they'll add their ideas for new ingredients to keep that improvement going.

Cassie: These meetings are going to stop at some point, right? It's not that I don't appreciate what everyone is doing, but I'd love to give this meeting stuff a rest.

Parker: Yes, at each meeting we can decide to stop, support you more, or help you with a new area. It's all about what the data say is best for you. At some point, we'll decide to turn it over to you totally, but that won't happen until you're flying pretty well on your own.

The agenda for follow-up meetings is simple:

1. Each member shares the data collected. If the data are consistently good, the team dismisses the case or decides to start on a new area of growth.

2. If the data indicate a need for adjustments, the team starts the brainstorming process again using the three columns for home, school, and student. Each person then selects a new action plan task. The team may also decide to invite new people to the next meeting, depending on the need for a different perspective or type of expertise.

3. If this cycle has repeated three or four times without showing evidence of student growth, the team may recommend that some forms of testing be implemented to add new information and possibly specialized services to the plans. This testing does not disrupt this meeting cycle; it simply adds to the data.

Tips from the Field: In Their Own Words

Practitioners had this to say about conducting successful student support meetings:

- "The makeup of our group changes from meeting to meeting, based on the needs of the student. Sometimes the classroom teacher, student, and parent are enough. Sometimes a fine arts teacher is just the person who can add a different twist to the plan. We avoid inviting psychologists and special ed teachers at the early meetings for fear we'll send the message that this meeting is about testing and placement rather than daily support for the student."

- "If someone violates the rule of no talking about the problem, the easiest way to put the meeting back on track is to ask the person to jot down their concern so they remember what they want to discuss after the meeting. If the parent insists on discussing the problem right then, we dismiss the rest of the team and reschedule the student support meeting for a later date to accommodate the need of the parent."

- "If parents don't show up, our teachers call and tell them how proud they would have been to see the way their child represented the family. The teachers report the meeting suggestions and selected actions. Then they ask if there's anything the parent wants to add to the parent portion of the action plan. Generally, this positive and supportive conversation is appreciated by even the most reluctant of parents, and we often see them for the follow-up meeting."

- "A helpful strategy for making the steps of the meeting clear to a student is to do a short role-play of the meeting, with the student assuming the teacher or parent role. Students who know exactly what to expect are less anxious and more helpful in meetings."

- "When we have preschool or kindergarten students involved, the process is the same, except for the fact that we give them the option to play outside the meeting room for about 10 minutes while the adults share their strategies. We then bring them back so they can select from their column of options and hear what the rest of us are choosing. This little break allows them to be included without boring them to tears."

In a Nutshell

One of the crucial conversations in this process takes place in student support team meetings. A flexible, tailor-made team is assembled to compile learning options that meet the student's DATA goal. As the student's needs change, the makeup of the team shifts to put the right people in the room at the right times.

This meeting is organized around two key principles:

1. Keep communication positive to produce positive results.
2. Surround the student with consistent and coordinated support.

Positive talk is maintained by following the rule of never talking about problems during these 25-minute meetings—participants only discuss goals and solutions. This keeps creative juices flowing, relationships healthy, and stress levels low. This type of meeting is possible when every member comes in aware of the focus and ground rules.

Surrounding the student with support is accomplished by engaging both the parents and student in planning as equal partners. The family is not at the meeting to just listen; providing their perspectives and ideas is part of the process. Because the environment is totally positive, it is safe and helpful even for preschoolers to attend. Combining family and faculty helps the team look at the whole child and puts everyone on the same page as they immerse the student in consistent encouragement and support. The cycle of coaching conversations, which includes student support conversations, continues until the students function efficiently on their own or until they graduate, whichever comes first.

We have now completed all the steps in the constructive conversations process anchored in appreciative inquiry and five whys thinking. You can use this process with anyone, gifted students and struggling students alike, whenever you feel the need for additional support in addressing students' academic or behavioral needs.

In our next and final chapter, we address some common questions that arise in conjunction with this process.

Questions Asked—
And Answered

Appreciative inquiry encourages teachers, students, and parents to develop a shared vision for learning and growth by implementing structured conversations that honor one another's ideas, life experience, and knowledge. Building this positive perspective into a school's systemic structure changes the culture to one that addresses both students' academic and social-emotional learning.

Research (Bushe & Kassam, 2005) shows that when people feel appreciated and valued, their motivation to improve and contribute increases. When a vision for the future is shared, relationships that inspire collaboration grow strong.

Here are some questions we frequently hear as educators begin this journey.

How Do We Get Started?

- Identify a strong leadership team at both the district and building levels to articulate and actively lead the process. Generally, this team includes central office and building administrators, psychologists, counselors, and teacher leaders.

- Make certain everyone understands that the primary purpose of this process is to give adults tools for supporting students' academic and social-emotional growth that will help them improve their craft through shared professional conversations.
- Explain how this new procedure resembles what people already know, how it fits into the existing structures, and how it will enhance what is already right with your system.
- Provide efficient protocols and time to have purposeful reflections so teachers feel supported. New programs that come with no resources, leadership, or time for implementation increase the stress levels of teachers and reduce their performance. The appreciative inquiry process reduces stress and increases performance when implemented properly.
- Think big, but start small. Make sure your leadership team can articulate the vision clearly for the long term as well as for the small steps they intend to use to get there. Starting small might also involve letting people have a say in how much and how quickly they become part of the process. This doesn't mean dragging it out forever. It simply means that allowing people to take on the amount of change they are comfortable with enables reluctant players to move at a gentler pace. People often choose to ease themselves into the process by
  ◊ Using the student conversation guide to get to know students early in the year and develop a relationship.
  ◊ Using the parent conversation guide for parent conferences and IEP meetings.
  ◊ Using the team conversation guide twice a month for team meetings so everyone becomes familiar with the thinking sequence.
  ◊ Sitting in on someone else's appreciative inquiry coaching session to get comfortable with the process and then following up by attending the five whys conversation.
  ◊ Volunteering to be one of the staff resource people to help brainstorm ideas during another teacher's student support meeting.
  ◊ Helping someone prepare a parent or student for the student support meeting.

To help this process along, you can

  ◊ Ask each teacher in the building to choose one case to follow for the year to pilot the process.
  ◊ Have one group of teachers apply the process during year one. They can then model the process and report monthly to the larger group in the learning year.

Activity 38. How to Get Started

Video 7.1. How to Get Started: https://bcove.video/2XlOf8e

As you watch Video 7.1, list reasons for making this change as well as tips for getting started from these two administrators.

Reflection questions:

1. Why would a school start a process like this?
2. Which ideas from these administrators make sense for your situation?
3. Who will you involve as you get started?
4. What small steps would you recommend for your teams for the first year?

How Do We Find Time?

- Work together to find common planning time for teams, as well as time for individual teachers to meet with a problem-solving coach. Teams can be composed of any group with a common open period. They do not necessarily have to share the same students or teach the same grade or content to brainstorm ideas that work for solving common problems.

- Some schools hire floating substitutes once a month who cover for a coach and a teacher for one period so they have time to confer.

- When an assembly is scheduled, the entire faculty may not need to attend. We recommend that half the faculty have time to meet while the other half supervises the assembly.

- Before or after school may be an excellent time to consider meeting because a wide variety of people are available. The downside is that this typically affords only 15 or 20 minutes. An option for extending the time is to do a time-trade. For example, a teacher may leave right after the students leave on Friday if he or she comes in 20 minutes early on Tuesday, thus carving out 40 minutes rather than 20.

- Brainstorm a list of things you can stop doing to make time for this more productive way of solving problems. There's never enough time to meet all the demands of educating students, so it's important to be selective and purposeful in how and what we schedule.

Activity 39. How to Find Time

Video 7.2. How to Find Time: https://bcove.video/2RA6fvV

As you watch Video 7.2, see what these educators view as essential for making time available for this work.

Reflection questions:

1. Would scheduling common time for departments or grade levels work best for your school, or would you need both, as Don suggested?
2. When would teachers have time to meet with individual coaches?

How Can Our Meetings Be More Productive?

- When teams have a clear focus up front, a structure to follow, and the intention to create a product by the end of the session, meetings will be productive.
- Establishing timed agendas and taking roles and responsibilities seriously are two essentials for keeping meetings efficient and effective. If the coordinator and time-keeper do their jobs, your meetings will always flow well.
- Administrators need to be active participants in team meetings so they can provide resources, support, and guidance.
- Always decide how to measure the results of what the team does in terms of how it affects student growth. That which gets measured and reviewed tends to get done with higher quality.
- The structured conversation guides in this book provide preset timed agendas that will help you organize problem-solving meetings.

Activity 40. Making Better Use of Time

Video 7.3. Making Better Use of Time: https://bcove.video/34A0MKU

As you watch Video 7.3, listen to both the administrator and the teacher points of view on use of time. What are the key points they make that enable teachers to accomplish more as people problem solve together?

Reflection questions:

1. What tools does your team need to give conversations more structure?
2. What would it take to make your team conversations more positive and focused?

3. What does your team see as the most helpful ways your administrators can support you in using time better?

How Do I Get Buy-In from Others?

- Valuing what's working now is essential to this process. When parents, students, and educators feel honored and successful, the desire to expand on those achievements happens easily without mandates, rules, bribes, or coercion.

- Self-assessment is where buy-in happens. When people discover for themselves what their strengths are, they are more willing to look at where they need to go next. If "how to make things better" comes from the outside, it's less likely to result in a highly reliable system.

- It's easier to engage people in expanding possibilities for improvement when you start with what they know works, rather than with what needs to be fixed. Every situation has something that works. Discussions should always start there.

- Have the faculty list things that currently work well for solving student problems. Continue doing those things, and ask what teachers need more of. Design this process so people see it fitting into your existing structure rather than as adding another process to their already full plate. People will nurture what they want to see more of.

- Don't end up with a process where people say, "I was told to do this." Design it so people say, "I know why this is important, why it works, and how to use it, and we have a plan and the leadership to get us there."

- Nothing breeds success better than success. Track achievements in small increments and make your data public. When people see positive results, they want to be part of what is making that possible.

- A key to maintaining positive attitudes is holding meetings around topics that focus on shared interests and common concerns. Topics that feel relevant and urgent to a group automatically generate the energy and engagement that move the group to action. That's why it's worth giving the faculty time to list what *they* see as the most pressing barriers to student growth.

- People must feel that the environment for these conversations is totally supportive. They cannot be afraid they will be judged for being candid or for suggesting an idea that may not fit traditional approaches. Make sure that each team member's voice is heard and that no one person dominates in meetings.

- Encourage teams to think like chefs, not like beginning cooks who must follow a predetermined step-by-step recipe. This problem-solving process encourages people to think outside of the box and create new and powerful combinations that support student growth.

How Can We Get Parents More Involved?

- Let parents get to know who you are, how you like to work, and how much you care about their child and family. Your self-disclosure invites them to share things about their family in return. Let them know that you want to hear about their goals, their needs, and what works at home to make learning easier.
- Give parents opportunities to be authentic collaborators, not just listeners or readers. Ask open-ended questions and focus discussions on ways to work together to make their child happy and successful.
- Display learning progress on growth charts that show even small increments of progress. Follow this up with what both you and they can do to help the child reach the next level of learning or behavior.
- Avoid using educational jargon during discussions. Jargon tends to feel condescending, whereas clear communication feels more genuine.
- Make your enthusiasm for helping their child visible through your positive conversations about what resources are available and your ideas for moving their child forward. That doesn't mean you never address problems. It means you never let a conversation end without at least one suggestion about what to do to *solve* that problem.
- Parents are often short on time, just like educators are. Think of multiple ways to communicate. Face to face is hard to beat, but sending happy learning pictures in texts and having short celebrations during a phone or Zoom call can get a smile and a vote of appreciation from parents.

Activity 41. Involving Parents

Video 7.4. Involving Parents: https://bcove.video/2XxJpsR

As you watch Video 7.4 of parent and educators, take note of what makes this process such a positive experience for parents.

Reflection questions:

1. What will you intentionally avoid doing and what will you add to your parent collaboration process to achieve the same positive results that the people on the video are experiencing?

2. When do you believe parents should be contacted for the first time during the school year, and what will be your purpose for this contact?

When and How Should We Involve Students in the Process?

- Teachers who overtly try to get to know their students show that they care about students, not just about grades and behavior. These teachers generally get higher performance and better behavior from students because of the healthy relationships they build.

- As Eric Jensen (1995) noted, punishment doesn't work with students who are victims of trauma, anxiety, and low self-esteem. We need to redirect students' behavior by having them set goals, create action plans, and assess their own growth.

- Someone should always prepare a student before asking them to attend a planning meeting. Helping them understand the purpose of the meeting and who will be there helps lower anxiety. Helping them decide what ideas to add to the meeting makes them feel more like part of the team than the person to be "fixed."

- Even our youngest students need to be part of setting their own goals and measuring their own progress if we want them to become lifelong learners. Preschoolers often only stay for the start of the meeting and come back at the end, but they should be there to help set the goal and add their ideas to the plan.

- Many times parents don't want their children in meetings because the child can feel victimized. If meetings are designed to build positive action plans, they focus on learning opportunities, not problems, which helps students feel safe and welcome.

- Getting to know students doesn't take a formal interview or meeting. Relationships are built in small snippets over time. Teachers who teach from bell to bell often think there isn't time in their day to have these personal moments with students. Teachers who know how to differentiate in their classrooms build small conferences into their class time daily.

Activity 42. Giving Students Voice and Choice

Video 7.5. Giving Students Voice and Choice: https://bcove.video/2Vt4C4n

As you view Video 7.5, list the reasons these educators give for making time to listen to your students.

Reflection questions:

1. When could your team find time to use techniques like the student interview?
2. Who should be conducting these interviews, and how often?
3. What do you think the payoff will be for choosing to spend your time this way?

How Do You Sustain This Work?

In school after school, teachers have stressed the importance of active administrative involvement. *If the administrators are not knowledgeable and involved, any initiative is likely to fail, even when teachers are highly invested.* Lack of support, lack of time to collaborate, and lack of consistency of implementation are bound to happen when administrators take a hands-off approach. When teacher teams were asked to define how administrators can help sustain this work, here is what they said:

- Regularly demonstrate and verbalize your awareness of the end goal and the road for getting us there.
- Recognize the demands this process puts on teams, coaches, and teachers, and let them know that you stand ready to support their efforts.
- Articulate the process to parents as well as faculty members and partner agencies. Be part of the rollout so the entire faculty knows you support the process. Remember that change is hard; people resist putting energy into something that is likely to disappear when the administrator's attention is diverted to a new trend. If you don't intend to support this, please don't start it.
- The time you're willing to give to an effort tells faculty where your priorities are. Implement a schedule that enables teams and individuals to access and sustain the process. Don't let other things push this to the back seat. If this is truly important, faculty members must have scheduled time for implementation.
- Check in with individuals regularly by asking, "How is it going? What do you need?" This enables you to see what training is needed and what successes should be recognized.
- Provide training to new faculty members each year, and keep the number of available coaches high enough to avoid overburdening the existing ones. This plan also addresses attrition of coaches over the years.

- As students change locations and grades, a system is needed for communicating to other teams and schools as you discover what works. Starting student cases from scratch every year makes no sense.
- Regularly solicit ideas for improving the process from staff, students, parents, and coaches. This communicates your dedication to quality and to sticking with it.
- Check to make certain that students who need to be involved in the process are not being left out. Direct people to the coach if a student's name repeatedly comes up as a person of concern.
- Explain how parents can get involved. Put the process in the handbook, and include it in presentations so parents can see and hear the steps.
- Make sure agency people who work with the school understand the process and how to get involved.
- Sit in on cases and meetings to keep yourself current on how things are going and what support is needed.
- Demonstrate how the process applies to and can be embedded in other initiatives. For example, use the conversation guides during "kid talks," department and grade-level meetings, staff meetings, intervention meetings, IEP meetings, and student and parent conferences.
- Break big teams down into subteams of five or six people for discussions and then share ideas among the subteams.
- Keep paperwork to a minimum. All you really need to keep on file are the final minutes of initial meetings and follow-up meetings.
- Appoint a coordinator so faculty members know whom to go to and to ensure things don't fall through the cracks. Also, give that person time to do the job.
- Model the appreciative inquiry process in solving building concerns as well as student issues.

Activity 43. Sustaining the Work

Video 7.6. Sustaining the Work: https://bcove.video/2wlfbbC

As you view Video 7.6, note the key ideas for keeping the process strong.

Reflection questions:

1. What do you think your multiyear plan might look like?
2. What mind shift do you expect to see as a result of embedding this process into your existing structure?
3. How will you measure the results of this work in terms of both student and adult outcomes?

Who Should Be Trained to Be Coaches?

- The best coaches are people who have earned the trust and respect of their colleagues. They know the importance of asking challenging questions that open people's minds to new possibilities while fostering feelings of caring and hope. They learn to ask questions that help teachers get into their students' heads and hearts before jumping to solve what appears to be the problem. Training a group of coaches to hold structured conversations that foster creativity, open-mindedness, and a "glass half full" mentality is crucial to this process.

- The more faculty members who receive training the better, even if many of them never serve in official coaching positions. The more people learn to think like a coach, the more efficient and effective the process becomes. Having one coach per grade level or department gives most faculty easy access to them. Ideally, the ratio of coaches to other staff members is one coach per six teachers.

- The system works even better when people have the option of talking to a coach of their own choosing. Being able to select a person you're comfortable with makes the process feel safe and supportive. Sometimes the choice isn't about the personal relationship but about who fits the student's case best. For example, the school counselor may be the most appropriate coach if there's a social or emotional issue, whereas a behavior specialist may be a better fit for a student who has high anxiety due to trauma.

Activity 44. Selecting Coaches

Video 7.7. Selecting Coaches: https://bcove.video/3ewp5OG

As you watch Video 7.7, note the qualities and tips these educators believe are important in selecting a coach.

Reflection questions:

1. How many coaches do you think your school will need to get the process going? How will you add to this group?
2. Write your own job description for coaches that will suit your situation.

Who Should Manage and Coordinate This Process?

The administrator is the keeper of the vision and the person key to sustaining any initiative, but he or she rarely manages and coordinates the day-to-day implementation. This is most likely done by a problem-solving coordinator, who may also be known as the Response to Intervention (RTI) or Multitiered Systems of Support (MTSS) coordinator. Figure 7.1 shows a checklist of tasks for the coordinator to oversee.

FIGURE 7.1

Checklist for Coordinator

Task	Thoughts
Help teams identify issues to discuss at team meetings that affect the learning of groups of students at Tier 1.	This structures team meetings so there is regular embedded professional development around quality strategies that address specific issues the group identifies as important and urgent.
Help teams identify a student watch list early in the year so no student gets way behind before receiving support.	In the spring, teams can send a watch list to receiving teachers. In the fall, ask the team to identify students who they think need additional support after the first two weeks. Start the coaching process for these students as an ounce of prevention.
Coordinate the matching of students to an appropriate coach.	Although the grade-level coach is typically the most convenient choice in terms of scheduling, sometimes a coach who does not teach on the grade level and is not familiar with the student is a better choice for the case.
Help the teacher decide how many people are really needed for each case.	The smaller the team, the more efficient the meeting will be, but don't sacrifice effectiveness for efficiency. New coaches may want an experienced coach to partner with them. If multiple teachers attend, choose one teacher to lead the interview and have the others be the "amen corner" to occasionally add to what the lead teacher says. This avoids the problem of people talking over one another. Too much conversation is more frustrating and confusing than helpful.
Attend coaching and team meetings regularly to identify strengths and support needs.	Use a tickler file to make sure you visit all coaches and teams regularly. Help them reflect on what is going well and what part of their process they want to strengthen. Follow up by connecting them to any training or resources they may need.
Keep paperwork to a minimum.	The district needs basic forms to track a student's progress and list effective strategies so there's no need to start from scratch each year. Make sure teachers understand that conversation guides and other paperwork are there to help them clarify their thinking, but they're not meant to be a requirement. Use the parts that are helpful in a sequence that is helpful.

The School or the District: Who Decides What?

Figure 7.2 shows nonnegotiables and negotiables that fit most districts.

FIGURE 7.2

Example of Nonnegotiables and Negotiables

Nonnegotiables Coordinated by the District	Negotiables Decided on by Individual Schools
Interbuilding communication forms, like the action plans and meeting summaries, need to be consistent.	Working forms, like the conversation guides, can be adjusted to the situation.
The district uses positive meeting protocols to support and build capacity.	Frequency and scheduling of meetings can be decided on by schools.
All schools have teams and coaches.	Who makes up the team and coaches can be decided on by schools.
Active administrative monitoring and support of the process happen regularly, and this feedback is used for reflection and improvement at the district level.	Who coordinates the day-to-day process in each building depends on what makes sense for that building.
Training is provided.	How to roll the process out, who will do this, and how to phase it in can be decided on by schools.
Consistent language for defining tiers, processes, and basic district forms is required.	What happens at each tier will be unique to each school's needs and resources. Schools may add paperwork to basic district forms for internal communication.
Parents and students are included in the process regularly.	When to include parents and students is decided on a case-by-case basis.
The process is used to support students with and without disabilities.	There's no wiggle room here.

A Bridge You Can Count On

Harvey Silver, renowned author and developer of the Thoughtful Classroom initiative, uses an analogy of a bridge to help people visualize the crucial components of any solid system. He says that each bridge can be unique in its design, but for it to hold together under pressure, its pieces must be closely integrated and aligned. It's essential that people can count on a bridge to bear the weight and stress with 100 percent quality.

The change system in this book is no different. It's a system to use at the first signs of trouble, when classroom teachers feel that their typical Tier 1, 2, and 3 interventions are not enough. Each school's implementation may appear a tad different based on unique needs, available resources, and the beliefs of the people operating it, but it must be aligned and integrated with daily instruction and school procedures. Because this is a process, not a program, it can be flexibly embedded into existing structures and expanded as needed.

Just like a bridge, this process requires three essential elements:

1. **A solid foundation.** We know that what we pay the most attention to gets stronger, so we need to focus on building on peak experiences and "I can" attitudes to get the most positive changes.

2. **Dependable support on both ends.** It takes administrators who set the tone by being highly involved and a faculty that follows through by adjusting learning opportunities based on students' strengths and needs.

3. **Consistency and alignment.** Strength and flexibility result from putting well-aligned processes and clear communication tools in place.

Thus the structure of this book. In Chapter 1, we described how this process focuses on the whole child in a significantly different way. In Chapter 2, we showed how the process lends itself to addressing issues that affect groups of students through teacher team meetings that quickly and efficiently design action plans to use at the Tier 1 classroom level. Chapter 3 looked at ways to use structured conversations to gather background knowledge from students and parents, and Chapter 4 demonstrated how a coach applies this knowledge to help classroom teachers develop plans that build on a student's strengths. Chapter 5 modeled a way to dig deeper to identify hidden needs that interfere with academic and behavior growth, and Chapter 6 explored how a support meeting that includes parents, students, and faculty can be a totally positive experience—when the structure is designed to do so.

Like a well-designed bridge, this process is a fundamental shift in perspective that connects people, opens opportunities and options, and reduces isolation to increase the effectiveness of the important work we do as educators. Most important, it's a bridge that will surely take us to better student outcomes. We hope that this book has provided the vision and tools you need to implement new levels of collaboration with faculty, parents, and students.

May the new bridges you build increase your capacity to support each other, the families, and the students you have dedicated your lives to.

Acknowledgments

Our sincere thanks to all the people who were instrumental in helping us develop this book. The wealth of knowledge and expertise shared with us and the level of encouragement given made all the difference.

Thank you to David Ries, Michael Searle, Linda Salom, Joan Love, Karen Spain, Ken Cornwell, Liz Wegner, Genny Ostertag, and Catherine Shue, who all helped us sharpen and clarify the ideas in this book.

A huge thank you to the people who allowed us to capture the work on video to give our readers a more authentic experience: Stefani Roth, Meltonya Wakefield, the faculty of Worthington City School District (Kelly Wegley, Dan Girard, Nathan Kellenberger, Lara Ruffing, Megan Kirsten, Bill Mosca, Shannon Howman, Tara Bogo, Julie Griffith, Michelle Antonchak, Meghann Moore, Brian Luthy, Laurie Barr, Keri Newcomb, Ellen Speicher, and Maddie Howman), and the faculty of Perrysburg Exempted Village School District (Brent Schwartzmiller, Don Christie, Rachael Sterling, Wade Kuns, Corinne Roach, Ashley Mundrick, Jamie Avery, Doug Pevoar, Amanda Reisner, Heather Rodriguez, Christina Temple, McKinley Kuns, and Brianna Chavez).

We owe a special thanks to the participants in our trainings over the years who constantly helped us fine-tune this process to make it more practical and efficient.

Answer Key

This key is simply an example of what a good answer may be; your answer may be just as accurate, even if it does not match the key.

Activity 6

Team Organization Meeting					
General Issue	**Specific Concern**	**Meeting Focus** (Skill we want more of; see strength charts)	**Criteria for Measuring Growth**	**Start Plan**	**Stop Plan**
Unorganized	Can't find assignments and materials	Help students develop routines and procedures for doing things efficiently	• Decrease in number of seconds it takes to find certain materials and papers		
Not motivated	Refuses to participate	Teach students to take on a challenge and risk being wrong	• Tally on-task behavior • Students can explain how they learned from their mistakes		
Disrupts the class	Walks around the room and shouts out	Help students learn to gain power, attention, and control in positive ways	• Tally walking and shouting (in one period, three times a week) • See if students can identify alternative ways of responding in class when things don't go well		
Failing math	Doesn't understand place value	Teach students to visualize and explain place value	• Pre/post showing or drawing of place value • Increase in correct responses with four-digit answers		
Can't apply phonics	Can't break words into small parts	Help students use consonant-vowel-consonant (CVC) patterns to decode	• Oral pre/post assessment of 10 nonsense words in context		

Activity 9

Accommodations: #2, #3, and #6 because they're teacher developed and controlled. The teacher or aide is doing more mental work than the student. Although accommodations are helpful, they're not designed to promote independent problem solving.

Interventions: #1, #5, and #8 because they require the student to make choices and apply a new skill to real-life situations.

Neither: #4 and #7 because one-to-one instruction is a group size, not a strategy, and does not describe what learning is to be taught or practiced. We cannot tell if what is being done is an intervention or an accommodation. Title 1 refers to a place or program to go to rather than a specific strategy that will be learned in that place.

Activity 23

All 10 ideas listed in Activity 23 have some value for reducing disturbances and increasing on-task time, but some teach Trenton the life skills of setting goals and self-monitoring that will serve him well beyond his school years. Research from Carol Dweck (2016) shows that teaching students to set their own goals and reflect on which strategies help them reach those goals is key to developing a growth mindset. With a growth mindset, students worry less about looking smart, so they feel more comfortable taking the kinds of risks that actually make them smarter.

As you reviewed the 10 items, you most likely selected the following as your top four:

- #3: Have Trenton chart his own number of disruptions and minutes on task (so he has data to determine what does and doesn't work).
- #6: Have Trenton set his own goal for how long he will work on a given task without a break.
- #8: Have Trenton keep a list of strategies that do and don't help.
- #10: Ask Trenton how he is doing on his goal and how he plans to improve tomorrow (reflect and adjust based on evidence).

It's not that the other ideas are useless. It's that they are more about outside control and support as opposed to teaching Trenton to change the way he controls himself.

Activity 31 (Scenario 1)

1. In the first question, the coach reflects the original concern of the teacher and asks why the teacher thinks that is happening.

2. In the second question, the coach allowed the conversation to switch to the executive function concern of paying attention. This is only OK if you go back and pick up the academic concern of not knowing letters and sounds later.

3. In the third question, the coach isn't even asking about Haley. This question focuses on the other students in the room.

4. In the fourth question, the coach has lost focus by asking about something that has nothing to do with the reading or attention problem. The coach should ask about what is going on in Haley's head, not how the teacher structures the room.

5. In the last question, the coach decides to solve the problem before knowing what the real root cause is. Moving Haley to a quiet place is unlikely to solve the attention problem, and it certainly won't help with not knowing letter sounds. The coach forgot the original concern.

Activity 31 (Scenario 2)

1. The first question the coach asked was fine.

2. The second question came out of left field. It didn't build on the teacher's previous statement. Because all students crave some type of attention, a good question would have been "Why does Jose crave attention by being disruptive?" Ignoring the comment blaming the grandparents was a good coaching move.

3. The third question was a why question, but the teacher wasn't getting into Jose's mind for the answer. He described what other 8th graders do that Jose isn't doing.

4. The fourth question built on the teacher's answer, but the teacher took the conversation down the "he needs stiffer punishments" road. When this happens, the coach should ask, "What would be another reason he uses class disruptions to get attention?" That's always a good way to bail yourself out of an unproductive corner.

5. The last question goes nowhere. If you end up brainstorming a list of punishments as an action plan, you've gone to the dark side. It would be better to ask, "What would cause Jose not to respond to negative consequences?"

Appendix A
Strength Charts

Attention and Focus

Knows What to Focus On

I figure out why the lesson or activity is important to me.

I look for ways to compare new ideas to what I already know.

I practice paying attention to big ideas and details so I can repeat them or make a list.

I block out things that might distract me by deciding when I can make time for the distracting idea later on.

I use movements to refocus myself (like wiggling my toes or sitting straighter).

Stays Focused

I break large tasks into manageable chunks.

I break up long work periods into small sessions.

I create games or competitions in my mind to make learning fun.

I know when and where to go for help when I'm stuck.

I keep track of how long I am able to work and set goals to stretch myself.

I have strategies for keeping up with the pace of instruction.

Makes Transitions Smoothly

I don't let fear of failure or unknown consequences stop me from trying.

I shift my goals and priorities when needed.

I create and use routines and sequences to move myself through steps.

I use self-talk and lists to make plans so I am on time and prepared.

I adjust my sequence or plan to fit new situations.

Shows Persistence

I tell myself I am capable of learning anything if I keep trying and I can name strategies for doing this.

I set goals and see the reason for reaching my goals.

I celebrate my struggles because this is how I get smarter.

I have backup plans for when things go wrong, and I adjust as I go.

I know how to ask for feedback when I'm stuck.

When I want to quit, I try to do just a little more so I learn how to persist.

Collaboration

Actively Participates	Is Dependable	Encourages Others	Is a Productive Group Member
I have strategies that help me stay focused and avoid the things that distract me.	I schedule my time in a way that allows me to meet my deadlines.	I listen to others and expand on or refine their ideas.	I help the group figure out roles and responsibilities for each person.
I make sure my group has a long-range and a short-range plan for the work.	I use checklists to remember what materials I need to bring.	I ask questions to make sure I understand the ideas of my group.	I make sure that tasks are shared evenly.
I provide useful ideas and research that help the group move forward.	I make backup plans for when things don't go well.	I am careful to include every member of the group in discussions.	I help the group compromise and come to consensus.
I actively look for and suggest solutions to problems.	I ask for help when I see that I may not be able to meet my commitments.	I maintain a positive attitude about the task and group.	I stay on topic so the group doesn't lose focus on the work.
I know my role in the group and make sure I do my job.	I constantly look for ways to improve.	I ask for and give group members helpful, constructive feedback.	

Communication

Is a Good Listener	Contributes to Discussions	Encourages Others	Stays on Topic
I listen so I can understand others' feelings, ideas, and needs.	I am brief when adding my ideas and comments.	I let my body language show my interest and appreciation.	I make sure my thoughts and ideas match the goal or topic.
I avoid interrupting or thinking about what I'm going to say when I am listening to others.	I present my ideas clearly and in logical sequence.	I notice when others need to talk and invite them by using open-ended questions.	I bring the conversation back to the topic when it goes off track.
I paraphrase or summarize key points I heard to make sure I understand before commenting.	I balance how much I talk and how much I listen.	I disagree in a way that respects the ideas and feelings of others.	I avoid sidebar talking during the conversation.
I make connections to what others say and note ways my experiences and ideas are the same or different.	I avoid repeating myself unnecessarily.	I share power by asking others to expand on their ideas and share roles.	I know how to paraphrase to make sure I am following and understanding the conversation.
	I am willing to speak up and share my thoughts and concerns.	I support my ideas and the ideas of others with facts, evidence, and examples.	I can summarize the main idea and supporting details of the discussion.
	I admit when I don't know, and I ask clear questions.		

Language Development

Draws on Background Knowledge

I visualize what I am hearing by drawing or telling about it.

I point to, label, or match pictures and objects to words I hear or see.

I compare and contrast new things to what I already know.

I retell in a logical sequence.

I fill in the blanks when reading about or listening to people talking about topics I am familiar with.

Is Receptive

I can imitate or respond appropriately to gestures, expressions, and sounds.

I can distinguish rhythm, sounds, and intonation that are the same or different.

I fill in the blanks in a conversation even if the background is noisy.

I repeat and extend patterns for sounds and words.

I respond accurately to statements by saying if I agree or disagree.

I follow multiple-step directions.

Is Expressive

I can communicate without using words through gestures, expressions, and imitation.

I imitate correct phrasing and sentence structure.

I visualize a story in its proper sequence and can tell it to someone else.

I can remember a song or poem so I can repeat it.

If I hear a sentence starter, I can expand on it.

I participate in conversations by asking and answering questions that match the topic.

Uses Appropriate Vocabulary

I know when it is appropriate to use formal, casual, or intimate language.

I categorize words, phrases, and idioms that have similar meanings.

I constantly work on vocabulary by using new words in my own conversations and writing.

I draw and play games to learn unfamiliar words regularly.

I try to figure out a new word by using the words around it, pictures, or roots and affixes.

Math

Applies Problem-Solving Skills

- I read and restate the problem or steps in my own words.

- I visualize the structure or pattern of problems and can show it with materials or simple drawings.

- I break complex problems into logical steps.

- I can think of ways to apply strategies to real-life situations.

- I identify the correct operation and useful data.

- I make estimates and can justify my thinking.

- I can identify what number is greater than and less than a given number.

Improves Fluency with Basic Facts

- I can demonstrate how to count on and compose or decompose combinations of 5s and 10s without counting.

- I do skip counting, doubles, and doubles plus without counting.

- I can see a quick image of arrays and create more than one equation showing how many I saw without counting.

- I can explain and apply place value with fractions and whole numbers.

- I do mental math daily to practice composing and decomposing numbers.

- I play math games regularly and can name the strategies I am using.

Shows Persistence

- When I want to quit, I try to do a few more problems or try one more way to solve them.

- I set personal goals and visually track my own progress.

- I give myself frequent breaks and then get right back to work to maintain energy and focus.

- I try multiple ways of getting my work done when I am stuck.

- I ask for help or resources when I am stuck.

Self-Monitors

- I see the real-life reasons for using math skills and can explain them.

- I know finishing first is not as important as doing good work, so I check my work for accuracy before the teacher checks it.

- I ask for modeling, guided practice, and feedback to check my own skills and accuracy.

- I can explain which strategies work best for me and my reasoning when solving problems.

- I give myself quizzes on hard math skills and concepts weekly to check what I know.

Memory

Takes in Information Accurately	Organizes and Manages Information	Stores Information Accurately	Recalls Things Learned Before
I set a purpose or goal for doing the work before I get started.	I look for patterns like main ideas/details, sequences, and cause/effect.	I create graphic organizers to see how new ideas are like the old ones I know.	I reorganize information in multiple ways over time.
I use eyes, ears, hands, and imagination to create mental and concrete images.	I find a way to get help when the pace is too fast or the material is confusing.	I ask for and give examples as I practice.	I think about how things are like what I already know and how they are different.
I see fixing mistakes as the best way to learn.	I balance my work time with short breaks.	I find multiple ways to remember ideas (songs, games, color, talking, drawing, etc.).	I look for real-life ways to use new information.
I focus on one job at a time, using about eight seconds to think before I begin.	I know how to break big tasks or information down into manageable parts.	I get enough sleep to allow my brain to make memories stick.	I think about what I heard, felt, smelled, and saw so I can remember better.
I block out things that are distracting me.	I start with the most important ideas and then add to and improve my ideas or work.	I highlight key words, reorganize my notes, or orally summarize what I know or what I need to do.	I know how to calm myself down to relieve stress.
I can stop one task promptly so I can work on something else.		I pace my practice sessions out over time rather than cram.	I use challenging memory games and activities to get better at remembering.
I compare new information to what I already know.			I test myself regularly to see how much I remember.

Motivation

Sees How a Task Is Relevant	Accurately Assesses Strengths and Needs	Sees How Effort Affects Success	Contributes to a Positive Environment
I can explain to others the importance and usefulness of the work I do.	I know my own strengths and use them to learn more.	I accurately estimate how much time and effort I need to be successful.	I recognize ways to show respect and acceptance for teachers and the group.
I choose to do challenging work because I know that taking reasonable risks helps me learn more.	I know what skills I need to work on, and I make plans for ways to improve.	I try to solve problems on my own first and know ways to get help when I cannot.	I make sure ideas and feelings of others are accepted and respected.
I work to meet my goals instead of working just for rewards, grades, and praise.	I know a variety of creative ways to approach learning and problem solving.	I look for a variety of ways to practice so I improve my skills.	I help my group get things done by working together.
I see how my effort and use of good strategies affect my own success.	I ask for help and feedback when I need it and know the right ways to ask.	I keep a list of strategies that do and do not work for me.	I ask for and use feedback and ideas for improving my skills and work.
I see how what I am learning can be helpful outside school.	I track my own growth so I know when to keep doing what I am doing and when to ask for help.	I use visual displays of my own growth to know when to adjust my strategies.	I thank people for a job well done and give helpful hints for improving things.

Organization

Sorts and Categorizes

I see and describe patterns that help me match things that go together.

I separate things into groups (by color, sound, shape, texture, use) and pick out things that don't fit the pattern.

I sort by more than one likeness or detail.

I sort important from unimportant ideas and things.

I describe patterns and rules for how things are alike and different.

Sequences Materials and Ideas

I can see the steps in my head or on paper for remembering directions, stories, or how I make decisions.

I rank ideas or tasks by how important or urgent they are to help me choose what to do next.

I have daily routines and procedures that help me reduce stress and find things easily and fast.

I look for patterns that will help me predict what comes next and can explain what clues I used to decide.

Makes Tasks Manageable

I break big tasks down into small steps to make things easier.

I know what I want to achieve, and I create a plan for how to get started.

I figure out how much time is needed for each step and create a sequence.

I make changes in the plan as needed so I can finish on time and with quality.

I keep track of information and materials using reminders and checklists.

I see how strategies I have used in the past can be useful in new situations.

Follows Through

I know why it is important to organize, and I see how it will help me.

I practice organizing things in easy ways first and then think of new ways that could also work.

I know what strategies work for me and which ones do not.

I have a system for double-checking how well I sort and arrange my things and ideas that I use regularly.

I know how to get help when I am stuck, but I don't depend on others too much.

Positive Relationships

Is Kind to Self	Cares for Others	Self-Regulates	Is a Decision Maker
I know what my strengths and needs are and set goals so I can improve.	I share my ideas and feelings with others so they get to know me.	I recognize signs of stress in myself and others and can use self-calming skills.	I can predict how I and others will react to a variety of situations.
I tell myself that it's OK to make mistakes and learn from them.	I help others without telling them what to do.	I recognize how my words and actions affect others, and I try to stay positive.	I don't share information that might hurt or embarrass others.
I take time daily to think about what I am grateful for.	I take time to get to know others by asking and answering questions.	I appreciate and support rather than complain and act cranky.	I try to see things through the eyes of others before making decisions.
I can label my emotions and say why I feel the way I do.	I make others feel appreciated and valued by listening to their ideas and feelings.	I ask for and allow people to help me when I am struggling.	I handle conflict by talking respectfully and directly to the person I disagree with.
I tell the truth without being harsh or blaming other people or myself.	I focus on what is going well and the good things people say and do.	I let go of negative thoughts when someone hurts or frustrates me.	People can trust me to do what I say I am going to do.
I speak up for myself without being rude or disrespectful.	I frequently tell myself to be patient with others and myself.	I admit mistakes and apologize if I offend someone.	I ask for and use feedback to improve my relationships.

Problem Solving

Makes Problems Manageable

I break down big goals or problems into smaller and more manageable parts.

I can visualize and explain what things should look like or sound like when I'm finished.

I figure out what information I have that is useful and what information I still need.

I can restate the problem or expectations in my own words.

When I am solving problems, I can identify what is going well and what I don't understand.

Creates a Plan

I set realistic goals for myself.

I sequence what I need to do by how important it is or what needs to be done first.

I look for patterns that have helped me in the past.

I estimate how long things will take and create a timeline that I check regularly.

I think of pros and cons of solutions before I decide what to do.

I anticipate roadblocks and have backup options in case I need them.

Assesses and Adjusts

I use models, rubrics, and checklists to self-assess my work.

I collect data and accept feedback on how well my plan is working and use them to improve my plan.

I keep a list of strategies and resources that work for me.

I stop to celebrate small successes along the way.

I see mistakes and set-backs as things to learn from, and I don't give up.

I can explain how my effort, skills, strategies, and decisions determine my success.

Reading

Figures Out Unknown Words	Expands Vocabulary	Reads with Fluency	Comprehends Text
I hear and distinguish sounds correctly and can match sounds to letters.	I use daily practice sessions to learn a few words at a time and practice for many weeks.	I use punctuation to make sense of text.	I think about what information I am looking for before I start reading or listening.
I can predict the word by listening to or reading the words around it or by looking at the pictures nearby.	I find new words and use them in my speaking and writing right away.	I read in phrases smoothly and accurately.	I can visualize what is happening or what is described as I read or listen.
I count sounds and stretch out consonant-vowel-consonant (CVC) words to hear each sound.	I use pictures, gestures, conversations, or games to learn and practice new vocabulary.	I read with expression to make sense of text.	I make predictions and ask myself questions as I read.
I use movement, music, color, and visual aids to blend sounds.	I use homonyms, synonyms, and antonyms to clarify meanings.	I set personal goals for increasing words correct per minute and track my own progress.	I frequently pause to summarize what I have just read.
I spell out dictated words by sequencing sounds using letter tiles or writing.	I use common affixes and root words to determine meanings.	I practice reading my personal writing to get better at reading fluently.	I can match main ideas or predictions to details and find evidence in my answer.
I hear and see patterns and can divide words into syllables.		I use word shape, letter patterns, and context clues to expand my bank of sight words.	I self-monitor to make sure the text makes sense as I read.
			I try to see how what I am reading is like what I know.

Remote Learning

Demonstrates Tech Skills

- I can use the keyboard efficiently, log-in, upload, and submit work online.

- I can find and organize work in folders and share my work online.

- I know how to participate in chat rooms and video or phone conferences.

- I can use e-mail and navigate the virtual platform and apps used by my grade level.

- I can use key words to find online answers to my questions.

- I know what to do when links don't work and other tech problems occur.

Organizes

- I understand the purpose of the lessons and put my tasks in order of priority.

- I break up long work periods into small sessions.

- I create daily and weekly schedules and routines so that I get breaks, attend class, and get work done on time.

- I use daily and weekly checklists to keep track of materials I need and tasks to do.

- I keep track of how long I am able to work and set goals to stretch myself.

- I set up materials I need and a place to work that helps me concentrate.

Communicates

- I participate in online conversations by asking clear, thoughtful questions.

- I listen so I can repeat what others mean or are feeling by paraphrasing.

- I share my thoughts and concerns online and encourage others to speak.

- I know how and when to get help when I am stuck.

- I look for ways to check my work and solve problems with online partners.

- I can define and explain technology terms.

Shows Persistence and Adaptability

- I know that if I keep trying and use good strategies, I can learn anything.

- I set goals and know the reason these goals are important.

- I keep track of my learning progress, celebrate my accomplishments, and adjust my plan as needed.

- I have backup plans for when things go wrong, and I adjust as I go.

- I know that my brain learns best when it has to struggle to learn.

- When I want to quit, I try to do just a little more, so I learn how to persist.

Resilience and Flexibility

Practices Self-Care

I use my body cues to know when I need to relax or find a way to get more energy.

I surround myself with positive people who listen to and encourage me.

I recognize what I need to work on and when to ask for help.

I reframe negative things so I can be more positive and understanding.

I make pictures in my head of what I want things to look and feel like so I can set goals.

I learn about how brains work so I understand new ways to manage my thinking.

Manages Emotions

I accept my feelings, describe them accurately, and plan how to respond.

I know what triggers my stress, and I know how to calm myself.

I accept responsibility for my actions rather than blame others and retaliate.

I try to imagine what others are feeling before I act.

I know how to recharge my emotional battery.

I know appropriate ways to get power and attention without taking them from others.

Responds Positively to Setbacks

I stop and think of options before I act or give up.

I use past successes as ways to solve future problems.

I see mistakes and setbacks as ways to learn new things.

I commit to small steps for reaching new goals.

I set clear and reasonable goals for myself and make a little progress each day.

Builds Self-Confidence

I identify my strengths and find new areas to improve.

I don't think of myself as a victim. I know what I can change, and I make a plan.

I develop plans and backup plans before I start something important.

I know and use strategies for shifting my own energy up or down to match the situation.

I adjust my pace, priorities, and strategies to fit the situation.

Self-Monitoring

Identifies Strengths and Needs	Sets Goals	Tracks Growth	Reflects and Adjusts Plans
I can explain what good, better, and best look like and where I am on this scale.	I set specific and realistic goals for myself that help me grow and improve.	I keep track of my growth visually so I can see what I am accomplishing.	I can describe what I did and why I made my choices.
I can list my areas of strengths.	I break the big goal into smaller goals.	I choose to monitor how often, how well, or how long I do things when I want to improve.	I can explain what I do to help myself when things get hard.
I frequently identify my own areas of strength and areas for improvement.	I can identify a sequence of small steps that will accomplish my goal.	I decide on tools for collecting data and recording my growth.	I can tell people which strategies work for me and which do not.
I can describe what I want my new strength to look and sound like.	I make commitments to an action plan and follow through.	I collect and record my progress on a regular basis so I can see patterns.	I look at my data and decide what I need to do next.
I ask for help when I need it.	I choose one or two small steps to start with right away.		I consider other people's opinions and suggestions for improvement.
I know what stresses me, and I have ways to calm myself down.			I notice and care about how my choices affect other people.

Self-Regulation and Impulse Control

Manages Feelings and Emotions

- I know the difference between my wants and needs, my actions, and my feelings.

- I read my own body signals and know how to calm myself before stress sets in.

- I name my feelings and what causes me to feel that way.

- I know what I need to do more of and less of to make myself and others successful.

- I know strategies for adjusting my energy level up or down to fit the situation.

Handles Setbacks Well

- I look for ways to help solve problems rather than find someone to blame.

- I use self-talk to slow down and calm down.

- When I feel like giving up, I come up with other options and try to do a little more.

- I know when I am bored or fearful, and I adjust my thinking and focus.

- I see my mistakes as clues to help me know what to learn.

Establishes Relationships

- I figure out how my actions and words affect others, and I try to improve things.

- I try to see things through the eyes of others (perspective).

- I practice good listening and using thoughtful words so being positive becomes a habit.

- I go out of my way to do and say kind and thoughtful things regularly.

- I ask for other people's advice so I can improve and make changes.

- If someone upsets me, I go to them directly to try to work things out.

Adjusts to the Environment

- I notice what is going on around me and how I can make things better for everyone.

- I predict what will probably happen for me and others when I make certain choices.

- I know how to gain power, attention, and control in positive ways.

- I look for ways to make things better for myself and others.

- I practice ways to adjust my energy level and communication to match the situation.

Writing

Develops Fluency (Gets Started)	Clarifies and Organizes Thoughts	Edits and Revises Work	Knows How to Improve Skills
I practice handwriting so it doesn't slow me down.	I focus on my audience and purpose as I write.	I use color coding or margin notes to see patterns, structures, and missing pieces.	I build self-confidence by keeping a chart of my growth and a list of things that helped me be successful.
I write nonstop for at least two minutes a day to get my ideas flowing.	I visualize my ideas in a logical sequence and use transition words to connect these ideas.	I ask for and use frequent feedback or modeling to improve my writing.	I know that it is safe to make and admit mistakes because correcting errors is how I learn.
I get my brain going by talking about my ideas, using a graphic organizer, or drawing my ideas.	I recognize and fix awkward sentence structure (run-on sentences or short, boring patterns).	I use rubrics to self-check or give feedback to others.	I know how to break big writing tasks down into smaller parts so I don't get discouraged.
I try to use new vocabulary words in my own writing and speaking daily.	I can distinguish essential from nonessential ideas.	I know resources to help me with revisions and editing.	I track the types of errors I usually make so I can set specific goals for improvement.
I sequence lists of my main ideas and details before I begin writing.	I use adjective and rich word choices to make my writing clear and interesting.	I choose informal work I have done the week before to practice specific editing and revising skills.	I practice fun ways of writing daily so it becomes easier for me.
	I support ideas with facts, evidence, and examples.	I use transition words to create variety in my sentence patterns.	

Appendix B
List of Videos

Video 2.1. Organization Meeting: Tier 1 Concerns. The Perrysburg middle school team demonstrates how to quickly select three team concerns to serve as the agendas for future topics for team meetings.

Video 2.2. Organization Meeting: Clarifying Concerns. The Perrysburg middle school team clarifies their top concerns and decides how to monitor student progress.

Video 2.3. Team Planning Meeting: Connect. The Perrysburg middle school team shows a quick way to energize team members at the beginning of all meetings.

Video 2.4. Team Planning Meeting: Focus and Success Stories. The Perrysburg middle school team uses success stories to generate strategies and see patterns for solving student problems.

Video 2.5. Team Planning Meeting: Design. The Perrysburg middle school team demonstrates how to generate a three-pronged action plan that involves teachers, parents, and students.

Video 2.6. Team Planning Meeting: Commit. Each member of the Perrysburg middle school team commits to a specific activity to get the action plan launched immediately.

Video 3.1. Student Interview: McKinley's Case. A 1st grade teacher shows how to adapt the interview process to build relationships and understand the student's goals.

Video 3.2. Parent Interview. A high school teacher demonstrates how to adapt the parent interview process to strengthen home-school relationships and understand the parent's priorities.

Video 4.1. Student Watch List. The Perrysburg middle school team triages the top Tier 2 and Tier 3 students needing immediate attention for intervention.

Video 4.2. Connect and Focus: Max's Case. The Perrysburg elementary team shows how to save time by starting every meeting with a positive mindset and clear focus.

Video 4.3. Success Stories: Max's Case. The Perrysburg elementary team demonstrates the use of success stories to see patterns of strategies that work for Max and the specific skills he needs to work on immediately.

Video 4.4. DATA Goal: Max's Case. The Perrysburg elementary team shows how to develop clear and measurable goals to guide the action plan.

Video 4.5. Design Home and School Action Plans: Max's Case. The Perrysburg elementary team selects specific strategies for home and school that will bring Max closer to his DATA goal.

Video 4.6. Design the Student Action Plan: Max's Case. The Perrysburg elementary team finishes the three-pronged action plan by selecting strategies that help Max become more independent and reach his DATA goal.

Video 4.7. Commit: Max's Case. The Perrysburg elementary team selects small steps for starting, chooses tools for collecting data, and sets up a follow-up meeting.

Video 5.1. Five Whys: Max's Case. Max's teacher meets with a coach to drill down to identify the root cause of Max's problem and uses the strength charts to target the new skill that Max needs.

Video 5.2. New DATA Goal: Max's Case. Max's teacher and coach demonstrate the four steps for rewriting the original DATA goal.

Video 6.1. Preparing the Parent for the Student Support Team Meeting. A high school teacher clarifies the purpose and structure of a student support team meeting in a way that makes parents equal members in the development of the intervention plan.

Video 6.2. Preparing the Student: Maddie's Case. Maddie's teacher explains the purpose and structure of the student support team meeting and helps Maddie come up with her three strategies to present at the meeting.

Video 6.3. Student Support Team Meeting: Maddie's Case. The Worthington student support team demonstrates how to hold intervention planning sessions that are 100 percent positive and makes school, home, and students equal members in the process.

Video 7.1. How to Get Started. Two Worthington administrators share ideas about why and how to start the process from both the central office and building viewpoints.

Video 7.2. How to Find Time. Administrators from Worthington and Perrysburg share ideas from both the elementary and secondary viewpoints on considerations for scheduling time for teachers to work in teams.

Video 7.3. Making Better Use of Time. Teachers and administrators from Perrysburg and Worthington share ideas of how the new structure of team meetings made such a difference in their teams' productivity.

Video 7.4. Involving Parents. A parent and two administrators from Worthington share how positive collaboration with families on a regular basis creates buy-in and support for both home and school.

Video 7.5. Giving Students Voice and Choice. A teacher from Perrysburg and a mental health specialist from Worthington explain the importance of active involvement of students in the problem-solving process.

Video 7.6. Sustaining the Work. Administrators from Perrysburg and Worthington share a central office perspective for how to get buy-in and how to maintain the momentum when implementing this or any other process.

Video 7.7. Selecting Coaches. A teacher and administrator from Worthington explain the criteria they look for before inviting staff members to become coaches.

References

Alloway, T. P., & Alloway, R. G. (2010). Investigating the predictive roles of working memory and IQ in academic attainment. *Journal of Experimental Child Psychology, 106*(1), 20–29.

ASQTV. (2016, March 23). *Five whys Jefferson Memorial example* [Video file]. Retrieved from https://www.youtube.com/watch?v=BEQvq99PZwo

Bailey, D. B., Hebbeler, K., Spiker, D., Scarborough, A., Mallik, S., & Nelson, L. (2005). Thirty-six-month outcomes for families of children who have disabilities and participated in early intervention. *Pediatrics, 116*(6), 1346–1352.

Battelle for Kids. (2014, May 8). *How educators are using vertical progression guides to transition to the Common Core* [Video file]. Retrieved from https://www.youtube.com/watch?v=AKbhYqmadNA

Blair, C. (2002). School readiness: Integrating cognition and emotion in a neurobiological conceptualization of children's functioning at school entry. *American Psychologist, 57*(2), 111–127.

Bushe, G. R., & Kassam, A. F. (2005). When is appreciative inquiry transformational? A meta-case analysis. *Journal of Applied Behavioral Science, 41*(2), 161–181.

Center for Teaching and Learning. (n.d.) *Engaging students in learning*. Retrieved from the University of Washington at https://www.washington.edu/teaching/topics/engaging-students -in-learning/

Collaborative for Academic, Social, and Emotional Learning (CASEL). (2005). *Framework for systemic social and emotional learning*. Retrieved from https://measuringsel.casel.org/wp-content/uploads/2019/08/AWG-Framework-Series-B.2.pdf

Cooperrider, D., & Srivastva, S. (1987). Appreciative inquiry in organizational life. *Research in Organizational Change and Development, 1*, 129–169.

Cooperrider, D. L., Whitney, D., & Stavros, J. M. (2003). *Appreciative inquiry handbook: The first in a series of AI workbooks for leaders of change*. Bedford Heights, OH: Lakeshore Communications; and San Francisco: Berrett-Koehler Publishers.

Durlak, J. A., Weissberg, R. P., Dymnicki, A. B., Taylor, R. D., & Schellinger, K. B. (2011). The impact of enhancing students' social and emotional learning: A meta-analysis of school-based universal interventions. *Child Development, 82*(1), 405–432.

Dweck, C. S. (2016). *Mindset: The new psychology of success* (Updated ed.). New York: Ballantine Books.

Fisher, D., & Frey, N. (2014). *Better learning through structured teaching: A framework for the gradual release of responsibility* (2nd ed.). Alexandria, VA: ASCD.

Greenberg, M. T., Brown, J. L., & Abenavoli, R. M. (2016). *Teacher stress and health effects on teachers, students, and schools*. Edna Bennett Pierce Prevention Research Center, Pennsylvania State University.

Hattie, J. (2012). *Visible learning for teachers*. New York and London: Routledge.

Henderson, A., & Mapp, K. (2002). *A new wave of evidence: The impact of school, family, and community connections on student achievement*. Austin, TX: Southwest Educational Development Laboratory.

Hoover-Dempsey, K. V., Walker, J. M. T., Sandler, H. M., Whetsel, D., Green, C. L., Wilkins, A. S., & Closson, K. E. (2005). Why do parents become involved? Research findings and implications. *Elementary School Journal, 106*(2), 105–130.

Ingersoll, R. M. (2012, May 16). Beginning teacher induction: What the data tell us [Blog post]. Retrieved from *Education Week* at https://www.edweek.org/ew/articles/2012/05/16/kappan_ingersoll.h31.html

Intervention Central. (n.d.). *Self-check behavior checklist maker*. Retrieved from https://www.interventioncentral.org/tools/self-check-behavior-checklist-maker

Isen, A. M., & Reeve, J. (2005). The influence of positive affect on intrinsic and extrinsic motivation: Facilitating enjoyment of play, responsible work behavior, and self-control. *Motivation and Emotion, 29*(4), 295–323.

Jensen, E. (1995). *Brain-based learning and teaching*. Del Mar, CA: Turning Point Publications.

Khan Academy. (n.d.). *Understanding place value* [Video file]. Retrieved from https://www.khanacademy.org/math/pre-algebra/pre-algebra-arith-prop/pre-algebra-place-value/v/understanding-place-value-1-exercise

Klemm, W. P. (2016, December 29). Thwart stress effects of memory [Blog post]. Retrieved from *Psychology Today* at https://www.psychologytoday.com/us/blog/memory-medic/201612/thwart-stress-effects-memory

Mayo Clinic. (2018, February 18). *Positive thinking: Stop negative self-talk to reduce stress.* Retrieved from https://www.mayoclinic.org/healthy-lifestyle/stress-management/in-depth/positive-thinking/art-20043950

Neason, A. (2014, July 18). Half of teachers leave the job after five years. Here's what to do about it [Blog post]. Retrieved from *The Hechinger Report* at https://hechingerreport.org/half-teachers-leave-job-five-years-heres/

Rowlands, K. D. (2007). Check it out! Using checklists to support student learning. *English Journal, 96*(6), 61–66.

Searle, M. (2010). *What every school leader needs to know about RTI.* Alexandria, VA: ASCD.

Searle, M. (2013). *Causes and cures in the classroom: Getting to the root of academic and behavior problems.* Alexandria, VA: ASCD.

Searle, M., & Swartz, M. (2015). *Teacher teamwork: How do we make it work?* Alexandria, VA: ASCD.

SLP Toolkit. (2018). *Accessing and using rubrics inside SLP toolkit* [Video file]. Retrieved from https://www.slptoolkit.com/blog/rubrics-video/

Smith, R. (2004). *Conscious classroom management: Unlocking the secrets of great teaching.* Newbury Park, CA: Conscious Teaching Publications.

Wammes, J., Meade, M. E., & Fernandes, M. A. (2016). The drawing effect: Evidence for reliable and robust memory benefits in free recall. *Quarterly Journal of Experimental Psychology, 69*(9), 1752–1776.

Wehby, J. (n.d.). *For students with intensive behavior needs, how many data points are needed to make decisions?* [Video file]. Retrieved from National Center on Intensive Intervention at https://intensiveintervention.org/resource/students-intensive-behavior-needs-how-many-data-points-are-needed-make-decisions

What Works Clearinghouse. (2006). *Improving mathematical problem solving in grades 4 through 8.* Washington, DC: Institute of Education Sciences. Retrieved from https://ies.ed.gov/ncee/wwc/Docs/practiceguide/wwc_mps_tips_072517.pdf

Witzel, B. (2009, September). *Visual representation* [Video file]. Retrieved from Doing What Works at https://dwwlibrary.wested.org/resources/472

Index

The letter *f* following a page number denotes a figure.

About the Authors

**Margaret Searle** is president of Searle Enterprises, an education consulting firm. She specializes in consulting with districts and schools in the areas of social-emotional learning, executive function development, differentiated instruction, inclusive education, and leadership team development, as well as in training teams to implement Response to Intervention (RTI) and Multitiered Systems of Support (MTSS). She is also an adjunct professor at Ashland University. Her teaching experience covers every grade from preschool through 8th grade in both a general and special education capacity. Her administrative experience has been as a K–12 supervisor, a middle school principal, and an elementary school principal. She served as an advisor to President George H. W. Bush on elementary and secondary education issues.

Searle's publications include *What to Do When You Don't Know What to Do: Building a Pyramid of Interventions* (2007); *What Every School Leader Needs to Know About RTI* (2010); *Causes and Cures in the Classroom: Getting to the Root of Academic and Behavior Problems* (2013); and, with Marilyn Swartz, *Teacher Teamwork: How Do We Make It Work?* (2015).

Marilyn Swartz is a national and international speaker. Her expertise on solving academic and behavior problems stems from many years teaching special education and general education students at multiple grade levels. She also spent years as a curriculum director and consultant for a special education resource center.

Today, Swartz is a consultant with Searle Enterprises working with school districts on RTI and MTSS implementation, research-based instruction that supports students of trauma, executive function, inclusive practices, differentiated instruction, co-teaching, and teacher collaboration. She also trains mentors for the Ohio Department of Education's Resident Educator Program and is an adjunct professor at Ashland University. She is the coauthor, with Margaret Searle, of *Teacher Teamwork: How Do We Make It Work?* (2015).

Related Resources

At the time of publication, the following resources were available (ASCD stock numbers in parentheses).

Print Products

Causes and Cures in the Classroom: Getting to the Root of Academic and Behavior Problems by Margaret Searle (#113019)

Never Work Harder Than Your Students and Other Principles of Great Teaching, 2nd Edition by Robyn R. Jackson (#118034)

School Leader's Guide to Tackling Attendance Challenges by Jessica Sprick and Randy Sprick (#118037)

Teacher Teamwork: How do we make it work? (ASCD Arias) by Margaret Searle and Marilyn Swartz (#SF115045)

Teacher's Guide to Tackling Attendance Challenges by Jessica Sprick and Tricia Berg (#118038)

10 Success Factors for Literacy Intervention: Getting Results with MTSS in Elementary Schools by Susan L. Hall (#118015)

For up-to-date information about ASCD resources, go to www.ascd.org. You can search the complete archives of *Educational Leadership* at www.ascd.org/el.

ASCD myTeachSource®

Download resources from a professional learning platform with hundreds of research-based best practices and tools for your classroom at http://myteachsource .ascd.org/

For more information, send an e-mail to member@ascd.org; call 1-800-933-2723 or 703-578-9600; send a fax to 703-575-5400; or write to Information Services, ASCD, 1703 N. Beauregard St., Alexandria, VA 22311-1714 USA.

THE WHOLE CHILD

The ASCD Whole Child approach is an effort to transition from a focus on narrowly defined academic achievement to one that promotes the long-term development and success of all children. Through this approach, ASCD supports educators, families, community members, and policymakers as they move from a vision about educating the whole child to sustainable, collaborative actions.

Solving Academic and Behavior Problems relates to the **engaged** and **supported** tenets.

For more about the ASCD Whole Child approach, visit **www.ascd.org/wholechild.**

WHOLE CHILD
TENETS

1 HEALTHY
Each student enters school healthy and learns about and practices a healthy lifestyle.

2 SAFE
Each student learns in an environment that is physically and emotionally safe for students and adults.

3 ENGAGED
Each student is actively engaged in learning and is connected to the school and broader community.

4 SUPPORTED
Each student has access to personalized learning and is supported by qualified, caring adults.

5 CHALLENGED
Each student is challenged academically and prepared for success in college or further study and for employment and participation in a global environment.